Amazing Food Made Easy
Healthy Sous Vide

Create Nutritious, Flavor-Packed Meals
Using All-Natural Ingredients

Jason Logsdon

Copyright © 2019 by Primolicious LLC

All rights reserved. Printed in the United States of America. No part of this book may be used or reproduced in any manner whatsoever without written permission except in the case of brief quotations embodied in critical articles and reviews.

For more information please contact Primolicious LLC at 12 Pimlico Road, Wolcott CT 06716.

ISBN-13: 978-1-945185-07-6

ISBN-10: 1-945185-07-4

Other Books By Jason Logsdon

Modernist Cooking Made Easy: Sous Vide

The Instant Pot Ultimate Sous Vide Cookbook

Simple Sous Vide

Amazing Food Made Easy: Exploring Sous Vide

Modernist Cooking Made Easy: Infusions

Modernist Cooking Made Easy: Getting Started

Modernist Cooking Made Easy: The Whipping Siphon

Modernist Cooking Made Easy: Party Foods

Sous Vide: Help for the Busy Cook

Sous Vide Grilling

Beginning Sous Vide

Table of Contents

Welcome to Healthy Sous Vide — 1

Sous Vide Overview — 3
Just Getting Started? — 3
Sous Vide Steps — 4
Sous Vide Safety — 5
Sous Vide Times — 6
Sous Vide Temperatures — 8
Sous Vide Equipment — 9

Recipes — 13

Morning Foods — 17
Sous Vide Porridge — 19
Cinnamon Raisin Oatmeal — 20
Oatmeal with Blueberry Compote — 22
Apple Bourbon-Maple Chutney — 24
Sous Vide Yogurt — 25
Broccoli Egg Cup Bites — 26
Egg White Only Egg Cup Bites — 28
Veggie and Gruyère Egg Cup Bites — 29
Avocado Toast with Hard-Boiled Egg — 30
Shakshuka with Poached Egg Blossom — 32

Soups and Salads — 35
Red Kuri Squash Soup — 38
Hot and Sour Chicken Soup — 40
Tortilla Soup with Shredded Pork — 42
Curried Butternut Squash Soup — 44
Creamy Parsnip Soup — 46
Turkey and Avocado Salad — 47
Duck Breast Salad with Cherry Vinaigrette — 48
Top Round Salad with Watercress and Kale — 50
Watermelon and Cucumber Salad with Cod — 52
Warm Peach and Blue Cheese Salad — 54
Tuna and Ginger Sesame Salad — 55

Grain Bowls — 57
Simple Sous Vide Grains — 58
Halibut with Melon and Wheat Berries — 59
Cuban Style Beef Bowl — 60
Chicken and Avocado Bowl — 62
Duck and Roasted Vegetable Bowl — 64
Shrimp and Quinoa Bowl — 66
Pork and Ginger Bowl — 67
Garlic and Parsley Lamb Chop Bowl — 68
Tuna Poke Bowl — 70
Harissa Marinated Tofu and Kale Bowl — 72

Main Dish Meats — 75
Filet Mignon with Roasted Brussels Sprouts — 76
Strip Steak with Roasted Cauliflower Puree — 78
Succotash with Hanger Steak — 80
Shredded Beef with Yam Neua Sauce — 81
Chuck Steak with Asparagus and Peppers — 82
Bison Strip Steak Carbonara — 84
Pork Chops with Broccolini and Peppers — 85
Moroccan-Style Tajine with Pork Chops — 86
Rack of Lamb with Brussels Sprouts — 88
Chicken Tikka Masala — 90
Chicken Mole in the Puebla Style — 92
Turkey Curry with Cauliflower Pilaf — 94

Main Dish Fish — 97
Sea Bass with Mango Salsa — 98
Mahi Mahi with Charmoula — 100
Swordfish with Bean and Corn Salad — 101
Swordfish with Romesco Sauce — 102
Lobster Tail with Tomato and Corn Salad — 104
Squid Puttanesca with Squash Noodles — 106
Citrus Cured Salmon with Fennel Carpaccio — 108
Halibut with Chimichurri and Tomato Salad — 110
Scallops with Tabbouleh Salad — 112
Soy Sauce Cured Pollock with Apple Salad — 114

Sides and Vegetables	**117**	**Equipment Links**	**145**
Beets and Goat Cheese	118	Searing	145
Sesame-Miso Bok Choy	120	Circulators	146
Dill Pickles	122	Containers, Clips and Racks	146
Spicy Rosemary Pickled Carrots	124	Sealers	147
Asparagus with Garlic-Shallot Oil	125	Other	147
Miso Glazed Turnips	126	**Cooking by Thickness**	**149**
Sous Vide Poached Cherry Tomatoes	128	Cooking By Thickness	149
Spicy Street Corn	129	Thickness Times for Beef, Lamb and Pork	150
Southwestern Sweet Potato Salad	130	Thickness Times for Chicken and Poultry	152
Cauliflower and Chickpeas	132	Heating Times for Fatty Fish	152
Infusions	**135**	**Cooking By Tenderness**	**155**
Orange Fennel Vinegar	136	Beef, Pork, Lamb and Other Meat	155
Blackberry Peach Vinegar	138	Chicken and Poultry	162
Flavors of Tuscany Olive Oil	139	Fish and Shellfish	164
Lemon Tarragon Olive Oil	140	Fruit and Vegetable	165
Cherry Vanilla Soda Mixer Concentrate	141	**Recipe Index**	**167**
Root Beer Soda Mixer Concentrate	142	**About the Author**	**169**
		Did You Enjoy This Book?	**170**

Welcome to Healthy Sous Vide

When I first got my circulator I made a ton of steaks, pork chops, ribs, and brisket and loved them all...nothing beats fatty brisket, finished in the smoker and served with French fries and macaroni and cheese!

However, more and more I've been trying to eat lighter meals that don't weigh me down as much. I'll still have a heavy comfort food meal on the weekend, but I don't need it every day!

It was a big challenge trying to balance using whole foods, less starch, and less meat while still keeping the flavor levels high and that is what eventually led me to write this book.

I still eat a ton of beef and pork, but I tend to use smaller portions and serve it with flavorful homemade sauces, instead of sugary bottled sauces. I also have been cooking more vegetables and whole grains, learning how they can combine to maximize flavors.

Healthy Sous Vide shares many of my favorite recipes that I've developed over the years so you can eat nutritious meals that still taste amazing.

I cover all the main meals of the day, with chapters on Morning Foods, Soups and Salads, Grain Bowls, Main Dish Meats, Main Dish Fish, Sides and Veggies, and even Infusions!

To be clear, this is not a "diet" book, and doesn't espouse any specific dietary guidelines. It is a book focused on using all-natural foods to create flavor-packed meals that will look and taste great.

If you have specific dietary needs, you can pick and choose the recipes that work for you, or use my recipes to find inspiration to create recipes of your own.

So if you are looking for hearty, flavorful meals that won't make you feel bloated afterwards, come on inside and let's start making some amazing food together!

Sous Vide Overview

Sous vide can be intimidating when people approach it for the first time, but once you understand a few key concepts you realize how easy it is to use. Whether you are looking to make convenient everyday meals that taste great, or you want to up your "gourmet" game and really impress your friends and family, sous vide is an amazing tool to have in your cooking toolbox.

Just Getting Started?

Trying to decide how much information about sous vide is always a tough decision for me. I don't want to leave new people out in the cold and confused about how sous vide works, but I also don't want to just fill up space that experienced sous viders will skip over.

As a compromise, this book offers a brief overview of how sous vide works and then provides links to my free online articles that look at these topics in much more detail. That way the novice sous vide cook can get up to speed while the experts can jump right to the recipes. So keep an eye out for the blue **"Note:"** blocks that will have links to more information.

And if you are really unsure about how sous vide works, I recommend my free email course which will step you through the entire process from start to finish at AFMEasy.com/HExplore.

Sous Vide Steps

When sous viding food, it almost always follows the same process.

The first step is to trim and season your food, just like you normally do in traditional cooking. Many of the same seasonings can be used, including spice rubs and most herbs. I usually salt my food before sous viding it, though many people omit it for longer cooks. The only big difference is that aromatics like raw garlic and onion are usually not used in sous vide because they will not break down with the lower temperatures used in sous vide.

The second step is to determine the time and temperature at which you want to cook your food. If you are following a recipe this information should be provided. If you are cooking something without a recipe, you can use the charts in the back of the book to figure it out for other foods.

The third step is to enclose your food to protect it during the sous vide process. This is usually done by sealing it in plastic sous vide bags but some recipes use Mason jars or other vessels. Most of the sealing is done using a vacuum sealer or Ziploc Brand Freezer Bags.

Then you place the bags in a water bath that is held to the specific temperature you decided on and let it cook for a set amount of time.

Finally, once it is cooked, you remove the food from the water bath and the bag, then finish it off by searing.

Once you've gone through the process a handful of times it'll become second nature to you!

Sous Vide Safety

Before moving into other areas of the sous vide process, I want to talk about sous vide safety. The main areas we will look at are the Danger Zone, Temperature Vs Time, and Plastic Safety.

I do think it's important to point out that sous vide is no more or less safe than other methods of cooking. There's a lot of talk about the safety of sous vide, but it's just as easy to make yourself sick by under-cooking a chicken in the oven or not pasteurizing grilled pork. So don't be intimidated, once you know a few rules of thumb you will be all set. And what you learn for sous vide is also applicable to all of your cooking.

Danger Zone

If there is one takeaway about food safety, it is understanding the danger zone.

The bacteria we are trying to remove during cooking thrive from around 40°F (4.4°C) to 126°F (52.2°C). They stop growing, but don't start dying quickly, until around 130°F (54.4°C). That range between 40°F (4.4°C) and 126°F (52.2°C) is known as the "danger zone" (cue Top Gun music) and it's often referred to in food safety circles.

Note that sometimes the danger zone is even considered to be up to 140°F (60°C) but that is based on building in a margin of error for restaurants, not the actual growth and death of the pathogens.

The longer food is held in the danger zone, the more likely you are to get sick from it. Most government agencies suggest that anything less than 4 hours is safe. Above that, it depends on what your tolerance for risk is, and whether or not you are serving it to people with immuno-deficiencies.

Temperature Vs Time

One of the things that is most confusing to people about sous vide cooking is why it is suddenly ok to cook chicken or pork at 140°F (60°C) when traditionally it has to be cooked to a much higher temperature.

The answer is we have always been taught that temperature is what makes food safe, but this is only half of the equation. What makes food safe is actually a combination of the temperature it is heated to, and the length of time it is held at that temperature. That time and temperature combines to pasteurize the food, making it safe to eat.

A piece of chicken heated to 140°F (60°C) and held there for 30 minutes is actually just as safe as one heated to 165°F (73.8°C) for 1 second. The reason the government suggests such a high temperature is that the pathogens are killed instantly at that temperature, but the same levels of pasteurization occur at much lower temperatures over longer periods of time. Using sous vide allows you to take advantage of this, since food cooked to lower temperatures results in much moister food.

Plastic Safety

A main concern of sous vide safety is cooking in plastic and whether or not this is a dangerous practice. Many scientists and chefs believe that cooking in food-safe, BPA-free plastic at these low temperatures does not pose any risk. The temperature is about equivalent to leaving a bottle of water in your car, or in a semi-truck during transport, in summer. This includes

Ziploc freezer bags, sous vide bags, and most food-safe plastics.

However, I find it hard to believe that we know everything about how plastic reacts to heat, water, our bodies, and the environment. As such, I encourage you to read up on the safety of plastic in sous vide and plastic in general and come to your own conclusions about the safety of using these techniques. I hope this will at least give you some various perspectives on it and you can make an informed opinion of your own.

> **Note:** For more information about sous vide safety, including deep dives into all of the topics above, you can go to AFMEasy.com/HSafe.

Sous Vide Times

The two components that determine how your food will turn out are time and temperature. All of my recipes give you the time and temperature I recommend, but learning about why I suggest them allows you to better tweak the recipes to your own tastes. The length of time you cook your food will accomplish three different things.

Heat the Food

At the most basic level, cooking is about heating up the food. Applying heat to food long enough to heat it through usually results in more tender, flavorful and better tasting food. This is usually how we cook steaks and tender vegetables.

With most traditional cooking methods, there is a fine line between heating the food properly and over cooking it. You need to pull your steak off the grill right when it is done, otherwise it'll be burnt. With sous vide, you have complete control over the food, and the timing is much less critical because you are cooking at the temperature you want your food to end up.

Make the Food Safe Through Pasteurization

Once the food is heated, we often leave it on the heat to ensure that it is pasteurized and safe to eat. This is how we traditionally cook chicken, pork, or hamburgers.

Pasteurized food has had the amount of dangerous bacteria and parasites in it reduced to acceptable levels (the US Government suggests killing all but 1 in a million, or 1 in 10 million, depending on the pathogen). Pasteurized food is then generally safe to eat, provided it is eaten within a few hours so the remaining bacteria do not have time to re-grow. Pasteurization is achieved by holding food at a specific temperature for a certain length of time, with higher temperatures resulting in faster pasteurization.

Pasteurization time is affected by the type of food, how thick it is, and what the temperature is.

Many people wonder when to actually pasteurize foods. Some foods like chicken almost always need to be pasteurized. All foods can be pasteurized though, and many people always pasteurize for added safety. It is also safest to pasteurize all food when cooking for immuno-compromised individuals like the elderly or pregnant women.

Tenderize the Food

The final step for some foods, after they are heated through and pasteurized, is to cook them long enough to become tender. This is critical for many tough cuts of meat, especially those that would traditionally be braised or smoked for long periods of time.

As food gets hot, the muscle, collagen, and protein undergo transformations that cause the food to get more and more tender. The higher the temperature the food is cooked at, the faster this tenderization happens. Many sous vide temperatures are very low when compared to traditional methods, which means it takes a longer time, but the lower temperatures result in a much moister end dish. Once temperatures in most meats go above 140°F (60°C) the meat begins to dry out and become blander. Using sous vide, you can hold the meat below 140°F (60°C) for a long enough time for the tenderizing process to run its course.

Note: For more information about sous vide times, you can read the tables at the back of this book or go to AFMEasy.com/HTime.

Sous Vide Temperatures

The most important thing to know when trying to consistently create amazing food with sous vide is understanding how time and temperature work together to cook your food. In the previous chapter, we talked about how sous vide times work and now we will look at sous vide temperatures.

As opposed to most traditional cooking methods, sous vided food is cooked at the temperature you want the final food to end up at. This is usually between 120°F (48.9°C) and 185°F (85°C), depending on the food being prepared.

Viewed from a high-level perspective, as meat is heated the components that make it up change. These changes result in structural transformations that affect the texture, juiciness, and mouthfeel of the meat. The higher the temperature of the heat applied to the meat, the faster these changes occur.

As proteins are heated, they begin to contract. This contraction squeezes moisture out of the meat, which is one reason well-done steaks are so dry. On the flip side, when collagen is heated, it breaks down, releasing gelatin and resulting in tender meat, which is one reason pot roasts and braises are fall-apart tender. Choosing the right temperature for what you are trying to accomplish is critical to consistently creating amazing food.

As meat is heated above 120°F (48.9°C) it starts to tenderize. The meat also starts to become firmer, but with minimal moisture loss. Above 140°F (60°C) the meat really starts to lose moisture as it contracts, resulting in much firmer meat.

Above the range of 156°F (68.9°C) to 160°F (71.1°C), almost all moisture is removed from the meat as it clumps together. However, collagen also begins breaking down quickly, adding a lubricating gelatin and creating a "fall-apart" texture.

This breakdown of collagen is why many traditionally cooked tough cuts of meat are braised or roasted for a long period of time, insuring the meat can fully tenderize. However, because of the high temperatures they can easily become dried out. Using sous vide allows you to hold the meat below the 140°F (60°C) barrier long enough for the slower tenderization process to be effective. This results in very tender meat that is still moist and not overcooked.

> **Note:** For more information about sous vide temperatures, including a detailed look at how it effects food, you can go to AFMEasy.com/HTemp or look at the charts at the back of this book.

Sous Vide Equipment

To effectively cook sous vide, there are three main pieces of equipment you need. Each piece of equipment comes in a variety of types and price points, and I'll give you a brief overview so you can determine what is best for you.

Sealing the Food

The first type of equipment is something to seal the food with. The three main options here are Ziploc Brand Freezer Bags, a vacuum edge sealer like a FoodSaver, or a chamber vacuum sealer like a VacMaster.

Ziploc Brand Freezer Bags are inexpensive and work relatively well, especially for cooks of less than 12 hours. I used them for several years with very few issues. Be sure to use Ziploc Brand Freezer Bags, or another bag rated for use in high temperatures, many generic bags are not.

Edge sealers cost about $100 and are a great option for people looking to move to a more robust solution than Ziploc bags. Chamber vacuum sealers are the most powerful of the sealers and cost several hundred dollars but they are worth considering if you regularly seal food for storage anyway.

> **Note:** For more information you can go to AFMEasy.com/HSeal for a deeper look at sealers as well as reviews and recommendations for specific machines.

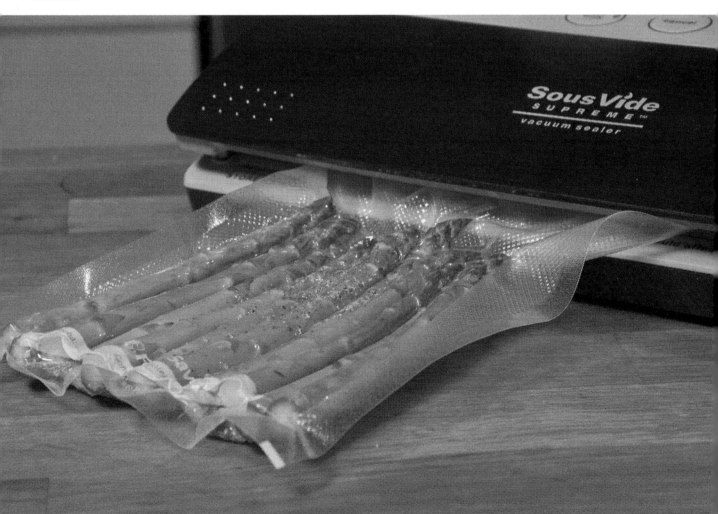

Heating the Water

The second type of equipment is something to heat the water. There are a few main options, but the most popular is a sous vide circulator. These machines go in a pot of water and heat it to a specific temperature, then maintain that temperature indefinitely. They make sous vide a truly hands-off process and many can be found for around $100. At the time of publishing, I usually recommend the Anova Precision Cooker, the Gourmia Sous Vide Pod, and the ChefSteps Joule.

For those just getting started, you can also try sous vide out on a stove or even in a beer cooler. These methods are slightly less reliable, and are only practical for shorter cooks, but they are effective ways to experiment with sous vide without spending any money.

> **Note:** For more information you can go to AFMEasy.com/HCirc for a deeper look at heating options as well as reviews and recommendations for specific machines.

Searing the Food

Searing after sous vide is a critical step for most types of food. It adds a level of flavor and complexity that you won't get from sous vide alone. It also makes it look much more appealing.

There are many ways to sear your food but the easiest is to pan fry it. It's the cheapest method since you probably already have a pan and a stove and is great for people just getting started. Many experienced sous viders rave about using cast iron pans as well.

I often use a BernzOmatic torch to sear my food. It results in less over cooking and has minimal clean up compared to pan searing. Many people use the Searzall attachment for this torch as well.

When I'm looking for more flavor, I'll turn to my grill to sear the food. You just crank it up as hot as possible before putting the food on there. You can also re-heat food in a smoker to add additional levels of flavor.

For non-uniform foods with lots of nooks and crannies like roasts or chicken legs, the broiler of the oven is reasonably effective.

Proper Pan Searing Technique

Searing is critical for adding flavor and texture to sous vided foods. When searing you want to make sure it happens as quickly as possible to minimize further cooking. Most sears should only take 1 to 2 minutes per side.

The key to a successful sear is to first completely dry off your food with paper towels or a kitchen cloth. Then heat some oil in a pan until it just barely starts to smoke. It's best to use an oil with a high smoke point like canola, sunflower, safflower or peanut. Once the oil is heated you place the food in the pan. After 1 to 2 minutes flip the food, give it another minute or two, then pull it off. The shorter it is in the pan the better. For some foods like thin steaks or fish fillets I will only sear one side to minimize the overcooking.

If you really want a deep sear, you can also let the food cool down before searing it. This will allow you to sear it for longer without overcooking it.

Recipes

I strive to make each individual recipe as clear as possible, but there are some things that apply to all the recipes. Please read through this before you start cooking so there will be no confusion!

Timing Directions

Many recipes say "cook for X hours, at least until heated through" or "cook for X hours, at least until pasteurized". This refers to the tables in the "Cooking by Thickness" and "Cooking by Tenderness" chapters. Those tables will give you the time needed for the specific piece of meat you are cooking. I do try to give a common range, which you can follow if you don't want to use the tables.

Timing Range

Most recipes, and the charts at the back of the book, have a range of time for when the food is done. For most cuts of meat it is important to remember that it will be "perfectly" cooked anywhere in that range. It is similar to ordering a steak medium-rare, we don't usually concern ourselves if it is cooked to 131°F (55°C) or 133°F (56.1°C), it will still be great at either temperature.

Salting

For most foods that are cooked I assume that you are salting and tasting the food as you go. Tasting your food as you cook it is critical so I recommend you do it often during the cooking process.

Common Temperature Ranges

In my recipes I recommend the temperature that I prefer but you should feel free to use whatever temperature you prefer. Here are some of the more common ranges I use when determining what temperature to cook food at:

- Medium-rare beef: 130°F-139°F (54.4°C-59.4°C)
- Medium beef: 140°F-145°F (60°C-62.8°C)
- Traditional "braised" beef: 156°F-175°F (68.8°C-79.4°C)
- Moist tender pork: 135°F-145°F (57.2°C-62.8°C)
- Traditional tender pork: 145°F-155°F (62.8°C-68.3°C)
- Traditional "braised" pork: 156°F-175°F (68.8°C-79.4°C)
- Extra-rare chicken breast: 136°F-139°F (57.7°C-59.4°C)
- Traditional chicken breast: 140°F-150°F (60°C-65.6°C)
- Mi-cuit fish: 104°F (40°C)
- Firm Sashimi: 110°F (43.3°C)
- Traditional fish: 122°F-132°F (50°C-55.5°C)
- Flaky Fish: 140°F (60°C)

Picking a temperature is as easy as figuring out what kind of meat you want and selecting any number in that range. Once you have tried out a few different temperatures you can get a feel for what you prefer. You can learn more in the "Cooking by Tenderness" chapter at the back of the book.

Obscure Ingredients

I try to make my recipes as nuanced as possible, but when the ingredients are more obscure and can easily be substituted I tend to suggest alternatives in the ingredients section. However, if you need to you can usually swap out the following with very little effect on the final dish:

- Vinegars
- Chile powders
- Finishing salts
- Olive oil for oil of your choice
- Paprika can be sweet or smoked

If your local grocery store doesn't have certain ingredients you can almost always find them online, either on Amazon or other online stores.

Common Ingredients

There are many ingredients that I assume you have on hand and don't call out specifically in the ingredients list for every recipe. This includes:

- Olive oil
- A searing oil like canola or grapeseed
- Salt and pepper
- Water

Sealing Foods

All timing assumes that the food is sealed in a single layer in the sous vide bag. If you need to use multiple bags to accomplish this, it is completely fine to use as many bags as you need. This is true both for meat and for fruits and vegetables.

Mixing Up Components
I put together these recipes with specific pairing in mind, but most of the proteins, sides, and sauces can all be used with each other. If the Turkey Curry sounds tasty but you prefer steak, go for it!

I also hope you tweak the recipes to meet your needs and fit into what you like to eat, or what you have on hand.

Keeping Food Warm
People often ask how to keep their food warm on the way to the table. I don't mention this in my recipes but I would suggest serving many of these items on a heated plate. This isn't critical to the success of the dish, but is a helpful tip I've picked up. I usually turn the oven on low and let it heat, then turn it off and put the plates in to make sure they don't get too hot. And make sure you use oven-safe plates!

Nutritional Analysis
We used NutriFox for our nutrition analysis, but due to a host of factors they are just estimates. If you are on a very strict diet, I highly recommend doing your own nutritional analysis to be on the safe side. Our analysis also contains only the required ingredients, so things that are marked as "optional" are not included.

Read the Whole Recipe First
Some recipes require curing the food, cooking for 2 days, or other steps that take time. Please read through the whole recipe before starting on it so you know you have the time to make them as well as have all the ingredients on hand.

Spice Rub Amounts
To make it easy to measure, I often overestimate the amount of spice rubs that are made (it's hard to measure 1/16 of a teaspoon!). So don't feel like you have to use it all, usually a light coating is best.

Morning Foods

As I've gotten older, I've begun to realize more than just about anything else that what I eat for breakfast affects my energy throughout the day. This has led me to cut back on the bagels, egg sandwiches, and Lucky Charms and try to replace them with food that will give me energy, instead of making me feel tired right off the bat.

Most of the breakfast foods aren't cooked "better" using sous vide, but to me they are much, much more convenient. Sous vide usually eliminates both the cleanup of pots and pans, and turns the cooking process into a hands-off one.

Grains

My trainer suggested giving oatmeal and porridge a try and I've really taken to it. My biggest issue was always trying to clean the pot after making it because oatmeal can be really sticky! Using sous vide allowed me to make it in a Mason jar and completely eliminate the cleanup. Plus I don't have to watch a pot since it's just on a timer in the sous vide machine.

I generally make a pint of oatmeal or porridge at a time, usually on some night after work. Then I chill the Mason jar and keep it in the refrigerator, heating up a few spoonfuls in the microwave for breakfast throughout the week. I'll top it with a little maple syrup, and some blueberries, pomegranate seeds, almonds, sunflower seeds, or flax seeds. So all week long it's really easy to make, super filling, and convenient.

If you really want to get fancy, perhaps for a Sunday brunch with guests, there are many upscale preparations for porridge. For instance, at 26 Grains in London I had an amazing burnt-butter, hazelnut and apple porridge, and my wife had a cocoa nib, banana, and date version.

Fruit Compote and Chutney

Fruit and vegetable compotes can be used on many breakfast foods, from oatmeal and porridge to toast or English muffins. They are really easy to make with sous vide and it eliminates the cleanup since the fruit is always in a sous vide bag.

There are many variations you can go with, but the simplest method is to just put some fruit in a sous vide bag and cook it at 183°F (83.8°C) for long enough to break the fruit down. Then you can smush the bag with your hands and pour the compote onto whatever you are eating. It can also be chilled and stored in the refrigerator for several days.

For extra flavor, I'll often add citrus zest, cinnamon or cloves, and some honey or maple syrup to the bag as it is cooking. And while it might not be considered "healthy", these fruit compotes are amazing on ice cream or brownies!

Yogurt

My wife loves yogurt and eats it almost every morning for breakfast. While it's easy to just buy some from the store, many yogurts are filled with lots of ingredients to make them shelf stable. Making yogurt at home allows you to leave in only what you want, my recipe only calls for milk or half and half.

I usually serve the yogurt in a small container my wife can take to work with her. I'll spoon the yogurt over berries or with some granola sprinkled over the top. It makes for a filling and nutritious breakfast that is quick to put together and easy for her to eat during her busy mornings at work.

Eggs

Eggs get a pretty bad rap in some nutrition circles, but more and more people are coming around on the idea that they are very nutritious and full of energy. They might not be ideal for people trying to limit their cholesterol, but for many others they can be a filling meal. Eggs are also an ideal choice for post-workout recovery.

Egg Cups

Egg cups were first popularized by Starbucks, and they are basically an egg quiche in a Mason jar. They are easy to put together and the sous vide process ensures they are cooked perfectly every time. You can use any combination of garnishes you like, alter the dairy in them, and even just use egg whites or a mixture of whole and partial eggs. For a creamier version you can use a blender to mix the egg mixture, or just whisk it together for a more rustic look.

Eggs

Sous vide allows you complete control over how you want your eggs cooked, ranging from runny, poached eggs up through hard boiled or even quiche-like. You can serve the eggs in many different ways, but I love them on whole grain toast with avocado, in sauces like shakshuka or a green curry, or in a grain bowl.

Sous Vide Porridge

Cooks: 183°F (83.8°C) for 30 to 45 minutes • Makes: 1 pint
Nutritional: Cal 184; Fat 10g; Protein 6g; Carb 20g; Fiber 4g; Sugar 2g; Chol 4mg

Porridge and oatmeal are very similar to each other, with the main difference being that porridge often contains multiple types of grains. This one combines quick cooking steel cut oats, quinoa, and bulgur, but you can use any combination of grains that cook about the same amount of time. I add some milk as well for a creamier result and top it all off with some pecans, sunflower seeds, chia seeds and honey for a hearty breakfast food.

For the Porridge
¼ cup Bob's Red Mill Organic Quick Cook Steel Cut Oats
3 tablespoons bulgur
2 tablespoons quinoa
⅔ cup water
⅔ cup milk
A dash of salt

To Assemble
Honey, optional
Pecan halves
Sunflower seeds
Chia seeds

For the Porridge
Preheat a water bath to 183°F (83.8°C).

Combine all of the ingredients in a pint Mason jar. Hand tighten the lid, making sure not to over tighten it. Shake up the Mason jar then carefully place it in the water bath. Cook the porridge for 30 to 45 minutes, until the water is absorbed and the porridge is cooked through, shaking the jar once or twice during the process.

To Assemble
Spoon out some porridge into a bowl. Drizzle with the honey if desired, then top with the pecans, sunflower seeds, and chia seeds.

Cinnamon Raisin Oatmeal

Cooks: 183°F (83.8°C) for 30 to 45 minutes • Makes: 1 pint
Nutritional: Cal 144; Fat 4g; Protein 6g; Carb 22g; Fiber 4g; Sugar 3g; Chol 0mg

Oatmeal is one of those dishes that isn't too hard to cook traditionally but I use sous vide for the convenience. I eat oatmeal almost every morning and I like to make a bunch ahead of time. Since you can cook and store the oatmeal in the same Mason jar, there is no cleanup of a pot and spoon, making it quick and easy to do. This recipe adds cinnamon and raisins to the oatmeal, adding bursts of sweetness and sharp background notes.

For this recipe I call for Bob's Red Mill Organic Quick Cook Steel Cut Oats because they are what I usually use. You can use any oatmeal you like and just change the time and water amounts. In general, it takes about 20% longer than is called for on the stove, and the amount of liquid needed is only about 80% of what you usually need due to the lack of evaporation.

For the Oatmeal
⅔ cup Bob's Red Mill Organic Quick Cook Steel Cut Oats
2 tablespoons raisins
1 ⅓ cups water
¼ teaspoon ground cinnamon
A dash of salt

To Assemble
Maple syrup, optional
Almond slivers

For the Oatmeal
Preheat a water bath to 183°F (83.8°C).

Combine the steel cut oats, raisins, water, cinnamon, and salt in a pint Mason jar. Hand tighten the lid, making sure not to over tighten it. Shake up the Mason jar then carefully place it in the water bath. Cook the oatmeal for 30 to 45 minutes, until the water is absorbed and the oatmeal is cooked through, shaking the jar once or twice during the process.

To Assemble
Spoon out some oatmeal into a bowl. Drizzle with the maple syrup if desired, then top with the almond slivers.

Oatmeal with Blueberry Compote

Cooks: 183°F (83.9°C) for 30 to 60 minutes • Serves: 4
Nutritional: Cal 157; Fat 2g; Protein 5g; Carb 32g; Fiber 5g; Sugar 11g; Chol 0mg

Fruit compotes, jams, and marmalades are real easy to make with sous vide. Simply put some fruit, with any pits or inedible skin removed, in a bag with some sugar and acid then cook it up to an hour or two and you are good to go.

For a thicker jam you can also throw in some pectin as well. You can make these either in sous vide bags or in filled Mason jars, but note that the end result needs to be refrigerated and can't be stored in your cabinet.

For the Blueberry Compote
8 ounces blueberries (225 grams)
Zest of 1 lemon
Zest of 1 orange
⅛ teaspoon cinnamon
1 tablespoon honey

To Assemble
2 cups cooked oatmeal or porridge
Fresh mint leaves
½ cup fresh blueberries

For the Blueberry Compote
Preheat a water bath to 183°F (83.9°C).

Combine all the ingredients in a sous vide bag and seal. Cook for 30 to 60 minutes.

Once cooked, remove the blueberry compote from the sous vide bag and lightly mash.

To Assemble
Place a spoonful of the oatmeal in a bowl and top with the blueberry compote. Add a few mint leaves and fresh blueberries then serve.

Apple Bourbon-Maple Chutney

185°F (85°C) for 90 to 120 minutes • Serves: 8 as a topping
Nutritional: Cal 79; Fat 2g; Protein 0g; Carb 10g; Fiber 1g; Sugar 8g; Chol 4mg

This apple chutney is a very flavorful topping that I'll often use on top of oatmeal or whole grain toast. It also works wonderfully on pork or fish. Sometimes I'll even use it as a savory topping on desserts. The apples are cooked in a bourbon, maple syrup and thyme mixture. After a brief puree they are ready to go. For a thicker chutney, or if the apples release too many juices, they can be briefly simmered before pureeing them to reduce the juices down. You can leave the skin on or peel them for a more refined presentation.

Depending on your final use of the apples, they can be cooked for anywhere between 1 to 3 hours. For this recipe I do 1 ½ to 2 hours at 185°F (85°C) so they still have some bite to them.

For the Apple Chutney
- 2 Braeburn or other baking apple, diced
- 3 tablespoons bourbon
- 2 tablespoons maple syrup
- 1 tablespoon fresh thyme leaves
- 1 tablespoon fresh lemon juice
- 1 tablespoon melted butter

For the Apple Chutney

Preheat the water bath to 185°F (85°C).

Place the apples in a sous vide bag, trying to keep the thickness of the bag less than 1" (25mm) for even cooking. Whisk together the remaining ingredients then pour over the apples. Seal the sous vide bag and cook for 90 to 120 minutes.

Once cooked, briefly blend the apple mixture to create a thick puree then serve.

Sous Vide Yogurt

Cooks: 110°F (43.3°C) for 5 hours • Makes: 4 cups
Nutritional: Cal 153; Fat 2g; Protein 3g; Carb 33g; Fiber 5g; Sugar 19g; Chol 2mg

To make yogurt you heat milk or cream to above 180°F (82.2°C), cool it down and mix with a starter culture, then let it incubate at 100°F to 120°F (37.8°C to 48.9°C) for several hours. Using a sous vide machine allows you to easily maintain the temperatures you are looking for.

Sous vide yogurt is typically made in glass Mason jars with the lids either off or not fully tightened. The starter bacteria will give off gases as they create the yogurt so a sealed container can leak or explode. The yogurt is also usually made in the container you will store or serve it from because moving it to a new one can affect the consistency of the yogurt. You can use the sous vide machine to reach both temperatures but I typically just heat the milk on the stove because it's much quicker than raising and lowering the temperature of the whole water bath.

I call for half and half, which results in a very thick yogurt. If you prefer a thinner one you can substitute whole or 2% milk. To get the incubation going you need to add a ½ cup of yogurt that contains live and active cultures. Yogurt that contains this type of culture will be labeled on the package. The length of the incubation time adds tanginess to the yogurt and can range from 3 hours to 24 hours.

For the Yogurt
4 cups half and half or milk
½ cup plain yogurt with live and active cultures

To Assemble
Mixed berries
Granola mix
Honey, optional

For the Yogurt
Fill a water bath to about an inch (25mm) below the height of the Mason jars you are using and preheat the water to 110°F (43.3°C).

Heat the half and half in a pot to at least 180°F (82.2°C). Remove it from the heat and let it cool to at least 120°F (48.9°C) then whisk in the yogurt with the live and active cultures. Pour the mixture into the Mason jars and seal each with plastic wrap. Place the jars into the water bath and let incubate for 5 hours.

After 5 hours remove the jars from the water bath and refrigerate until chilled. Once the yogurt is cold, seal with the Mason jar lids. It will last in the refrigerator for 1 to 2 weeks.

To Assemble
Place some berries in a bowl and cover with a spoonful or two of the yogurt. Top with some granola mix and drizzle some honey on top.

Broccoli Egg Cup Bites

Cooks: 170°F (76.6°C) for 1 hour • Serves: 4
Nutritional: Cal 287; Fat 23g; Protein 15g; Carb 7g; Fiber 1g; Sugar 3g; Chol 327mg

These egg cup bites were first popularized by Starbucks but are really easy to make at home. You can use any ingredients you want to flavor them but I always enjoy broccoli and cheddar cheese. For a lighter egg you can replace the cream with milk, or use ¼ cup cream cheese for a denser end result.

You can make them in any glass container but a ¼ pint or ½ pint works really well, just make sure to only finger-tighten the lid so the gases can escape. I've also made them in ramekins which create a unique shape for the egg. These egg bites will last in the refrigerator for about a week without losing any quality.

For the Eggs
6 eggs
½ cup shredded cheddar cheese
½ cup heavy cream
A dash of salt and pepper
½ cup diced cooked broccoli
½ cup cooked sliced shallots

For the Eggs
Preheat a water bath to 170°F (76.6°C).

Whisk or blend together the eggs, cheese, cream, salt and pepper. Evenly distribute the remaining ingredients between your Mason jars. Add the egg mixture evenly to the jars then finger tighten the lids. Shake the jars well so the ingredients will combine. Place in the water bath and cook for 60 minutes.

Remove from the water bath and serve by running a knife along the inside of the jar.

Egg White Only Egg Cup Bites

Cooks: 170°F (76.6°C) for 1 hour • Serves: 4
Nutritional: Cal 109; Fat 3g; Protein 16g; Carb 5g; Fiber 0g; Sugar 4g; Chol 23mg

I put this recipe together for those people who are trying to limit the amount of egg yolk they consume. It uses only egg whites, cottage cheese, and milk to form the base of the dish. You can make any of the other egg cups using only egg whites, or a combination of egg whites and yolks.

This egg cup is filled out with spinach and flavorful bursts of sun dried tomatoes. Note that the spinach is wilted before you put it in the jar. If you use fresh spinach the water it releases will make the eggs runny. For extra flavor, you can top them with grated cheese and melt it.

For the Eggs
- 8 eggs, yolks removed
- ½ cup cottage cheese
- ½ cup milk
- A dash of salt and pepper
- ½ cup wilted spinach
- 3 tablespoons chopped sun dried tomatoes
- ½ cup diced cooked turkey

For the Eggs

Preheat a water bath to 170°F (76.6°C).

Whisk or blend together the eggs, cheese, milk, salt and pepper in a bowl. Evenly distribute the remaining ingredients between your Mason jars. Add the egg mixture evenly to the jars then finger tighten the lids. Shake the jars well so the ingredients will combine. Place in the water bath and cook for 60 minutes.

Remove from the water bath and serve by running a knife along the inside of the jar.

Veggie and Gruyère Egg Cup Bites

Cooks: 170°F (76.6°C) for 1 hour • Serves: 4
Nutritional: Cal 276; Fat 22g; Protein 15g; Carb 4g; Fiber 1g; Sugar 3g; Chol 325mg

To showcase how versatile they are, I've taken these egg cup bites in a different direction by using tangy Gruyère cheese and hearty peppers, mushrooms and tomatoes. I also replaced some of the heavy cream with cream cheese for a denser egg bite. Like all egg bites, you can serve them in the container or remove them and serve them on a plate. For an extra-fancy presentation I plate them then give them a sear with my torch for added color and flavor.

For the Eggs
6 eggs
½ cup shredded Gruyère cheese
¼ cup cream cheese
¼ cup heavy cream
A dash of salt and pepper
½ cup diced bell peppers
½ cup diced mushrooms
½ cup cherry tomato halves

For the Eggs
Preheat a water bath to 170°F (76.6°C).

Whisk or blend together the eggs, cheeses, cream, salt and pepper in a bowl. Evenly distribute the remaining ingredients between your Mason jars. Add the egg mixture evenly to the jars then finger tighten the lids. Shake the jars well so the ingredients will combine. Place in the water bath and cook for 60 minutes.

Remove from the water bath and serve by running a knife along the inside of the jar.

Avocado Toast with Hard-Boiled Egg

Cooks: 165°F (73.8°C) for 40 to 60 minutes • Serves: 4
Nutritional: Cal 423; Fat 29g; Protein 15g; Carb 30g; Fiber 12g; Sugar 7g; Chol 186mg

Avocado toast is all the rage lately and I can see why. A piece of hearty, whole grain bread lightly toasted and slathered with rich and creamy avocado is a decadent combination. I especially love it when topped with an egg to make it a complete meal. Be sure to use a high-quality bread and a ripe avocado, because this recipe is so simple the flavors will really shine through.

This recipe calls for a hard-boiled egg but many people also like using a runny poached or fried egg, so feel free to use whichever you prefer.

For the Hard-Boiled Egg
4 eggs

For the Avocado Spread
2 avocados
2 tablespoons olive oil
Fresh lime juice

To Assemble
4 slices of whole grain bread, toasted
Fresh basil leaves, chopped
Freshly cracked black pepper
Sea salt

For the Hard-Boiled Egg
Preheat the water bath to 165°F (73.8°C).

Place the eggs, in the shells, directly in the water bath and cook for 40 to 60 minutes.

For the Avocado Spread
Remove the flesh from the avocado and mash together with the olive oil. Add the lime juice, salt and pepper to taste until it is slightly tangy and well balanced.

To Assemble
Remove the eggs from their shells and cut into ½" slices (13mm).

Take a slice of toasted bread and slather on some of the avocado spread. Add slices of the hard-boiled eggs to the toast then sprinkle with the basil, fresh cracked pepper, and sea salt.

Shakshuka with Poached Egg Blossom

Cooks: 167°F (75.0°C) for 10 to 15 minutes • Serves: 4
Nutritional: Cal 319; Fat 8g; Protein 16g; Carb 51g; Fiber 8g; Sugar 10g; Chol 186mg

I first tried shakshuka at the Park Slope restaurant Miriam, which serves an amazing variety of Israeli foods for brunch. It's a hearty and filling meal that is still packed with fresh ingredients prepared simply. I try to use fresh tomatoes from the farmers market, but you can use high-quality canned ones as well.

Traditionally, the eggs are poached in the shakshuka but I've found making them in the sous vide machine adds a level of control to the process that I didn't have before. I like to use *Modernist Cuisine*'s technique to make egg blossoms before poaching them, which removes the difficulty of getting them out of the shell and also results in a unique look. Feel free to just cook them in the shell if you prefer.

For the Egg Blossoms
4 eggs

For the Shakshuka
½ yellow onion, diced
3 cloves garlic, minced
1 red bell pepper, diced
6 plum tomatoes, diced
1 ½ cups crushed tomatoes
2 teaspoons paprika
1 teaspoon ground cumin
1 teaspoon ground coriander
⅛ teaspoon cayenne pepper powder
1 bay leaf

To Assemble
Fresh parsley, chopped
Pita bread

For the Egg Blossoms
Preheat the water bath to 167°F (75.0°C).

Place some plastic wrap in a small bowl and lightly brush the middle with olive oil then crack an egg into it. Salt and pepper the egg. Pull the corners of the plastic wrap up and twist the bottom of the plastic to form a ball, removing all the air, then tie to secure it. Repeat for the remaining eggs.

Place the blossom pouches in the water bath and cook until the white is set, about 10 to 15 minutes, depending on the size of the egg.

For the Shakshuka
Heat some olive oil in a pan over medium-high heat. Add the onion and cook until softened, about 10 to 15 minutes, stirring occasionally. Add the minced garlic and red pepper and cook for 5 minutes. Add the plum tomatoes and their juices then stir well to combine and cook for 5 to 10 minutes. Add the crushed tomatoes, as well as the spices and bay leaf, then stir well to combine. If the tomatoes don't have much juice, you may need to add some water or balsamic vinegar to prevent them from drying out.

Let cook until it has thickened slightly, the vegetables have broken down, and the flavors have melded, about 15 to 30 minutes. Remove the bay leaf. If you prefer a less chunky shakshuka you can puree the resulting mixture in a blender or food processor.

To Assemble
Fill a bowl with the shakshuka. Cut the plastic wrap off of an egg and place it in the bowl. Sprinkle with the parsley and serve with pita bread.

Soups and Salads

Sometimes the day calls for a crisp, flavorful salad or a warm bowl of hearty soup. In my quest to cut down on eating out, I've been making more soups and salads, but I still want them full of rich flavors and to be really filling. Using sous vide allows me to easily add perfectly cooked meat and vegetables to these with very little effort.

Soups

At their most basic, soups are flavorful infusions of meat and vegetables. At their worst, they are filled with starches, preservatives, and tons of salt. The recipes in this chapter are bold and full of flavor, using fresh ingredients to fill them with nutrition. Taking the time to make these soups at home is also worth the effort so you know exactly what is in them.

Most soups are also a perfect candidate for freezing. You store them in smaller, serving-sized containers and then quickly reheat them later.

Pureed Soups

One of the easiest ways to use sous vide is to make pureed soups. It's one of the uses where the results might not be any better than using the stovetop, but sous vide makes it so much more convenient.

The pureed soups in this chapter all are fully cooked in the sous vide bag, meaning you don't have to try and scrub scorched soup off of a pot. These types of pureed soups work with many different kinds of vegetables and allow you a wide variety of flavoring combinations. In addition to the recipes here, I also really like puree soup made from carrots, cauliflower, sweet potato, turnips, and beets.

Meat-Based Soups

Many soups contain pieces of meat in them, and sous vide shines when you want to ensure it is cooked perfectly. We have all had a rich, filling soup ruined by dry pieces of meat. Sous viding the meat separately ensures it is tender and moist, adding to the soup instead of taking away from it.

I've given recipes for two of my favorite meat-based soups in this chapter. Feel free to substitute other types of meat if you prefer, or even just some crunchy vegetables.

One important tip for meat-based soups is to make sure you use high quality stock in them. With a traditional soup, the cooking process pulls flavor out of the meat into the liquid, so you can get away with a lower quality stock. But with sous vide, all the flavor of the meat stays in the meat, so the liquid can taste bland if it is not high quality already. I highly recommend making your own stocks at home. They are very easy to do, simple to freeze, and impart rich flavors into your dishes. To learn more about making stock I recommend Michael Ruhlman's series of articles on it: ruhlman.com/2015/01/meat-broths-and-stock.

Salads

A big part of a nutritious life style is making sure you are eating enough salads. I often struggle with salad and it's not something I crave. I've worked hard to come up with salads that are not only chock full of lettuce and vegetables but are really filling. This chapter contains some of my got-to salads. I would still prefer a juicy hamburger, but these recipes make it easier for me to behave...at least most of the time!

Salads with Meat

There's nothing wrong with a simple side salad, but for a hearty meal I need to have meat with my lettuce! Ensuring the meat is moist and adds to the salad is very important, and sous vide makes it easy.

Sous vide is also very convenient for several reasons. I'll often make several batches of meat ahead of time and store the rest in the fridge or freezer until I need it. You can do this at any point in the process, either before cooking it, or after cooking it but before searing it. If it is after sous viding it, just chill it in an ice bath for 15 to 20 minutes to fully chill the meat then toss them in the fridge or freezer.

Another way to optimize the process is to skip the sear unless you are trying to be fancy. I almost never sear my poultry and even skip it on some meat. It's not as pretty, but for a quick and nutritious lunch anything to speed up the process helps to keep me from reaching for unhealthy food.

> **Note:** In these recipes I recommend the time and temperatures I prefer, but for more options you can refer to the "Common Temperature Ranges" section at the start of the "Recipes" chapter or the "Cooking by Tenderness" chapter.

Red Kuri Squash Soup

Cooks: 183°F (83.9°C) for 1 to 4 hours • Serves: 4
Nutritional: Cal 122; Fat 8g; Protein 2g; Carb 14g; Fiber 3g; Sugar 4g; Chol 8mg

Red kuri squash is a nutty and sweet winter squash. It can be used in most dishes that call for butternut squash or pumpkin and it is a favorite of mine to use in late fall. Cooking it with sous vide makes it an easy process with very little cleanup at the end.

Since you will be pureeing the squash you want to make sure it's nice and soft. I often cook it until it is relatively easy to squeeze through the bag. You can serve this by itself, as the first course of a big meal, or with some hearty bread.

For the Red Kuri Squash
1 medium red kuri squash, about 2 pounds (900 grams)
2 cloves garlic, coarsely chopped
1 shallot, coarsely chopped
1 tablespoon olive oil or butter
⅛ teaspoon ground cloves
¼ teaspoon allspice
1 tablespoon brown sugar, optional
⅔ cup vegetable broth or chicken stock
2 tablespoons white wine vinegar

To Assemble
¼ cup pecan halves
1 shallot, thinly sliced
1 lime
Fresh basil leaves

For the Red Kuri Squash
Preheat a water bath to 183°F (83.9°C).

Peel the red kuri squash then cut in half and remove the seeds. Cut the flesh into ½" chunks (13mm). You should have about 2 cups.

Place the cubed squash into one or two sous vide bags, making sure it is in a single layer. Add the garlic, shallot, olive oil, cloves, allspice, and brown sugar to the sous vide bag. Seal the bag and cook for at least an hour, but preferably 2 to 3.

Once cooked, remove the squash from the sous vide bag and place in a blender or food processor. Add the vegetable broth and white wine vinegar then blend until fully pureed. Salt and pepper to taste.

To Assemble
Place the pecan halves in a pan without oil and cook over medium heat until lightly browned, stirring often. Remove the pecans from the heat and set aside.

Heat some olive oil in a pan over medium heat. Add the sliced shallots and cook until they turn translucent and just start to brown. Remove from the heat and set aside.

Place a ladle or two of the soup into a bowl then top with some pecans and shallots. Zest some lime over the top and add a basil leaf or two then serve.

Hot and Sour Chicken Soup

Cooks: 141°F (60.5°C) for 2 to 4 hours • Serves: 4
Nutritional: Cal 291; Fat 6g; Protein 34g; Carb 23g; Fiber 2g; Sugar 6g; Chol 90mg

I recently took a Thai cooking class at the Institute of Culinary Education in Manhattan and ever since I've been trying to work traditional Thai flavors into my cooking. Classic Thai food has an amazing mix of hot, salty, and sour and I tried to work that into this flavorful soup. The soup pops in your mouth, with bright highs of all the flavor combinations.

The lemongrass and kaffir lime leaves might be hard to find in your area but they can both be ordered online from Amazon.com and stored in the refrigerator for months. I used peas, carrots, mushrooms, and collard greens but go ahead and substitute anything tasty you have around the house. You can also use pork, beef, or shrimp instead of the chicken if you prefer.

For the Chicken
2 chicken breasts

For the Hot and Sour Soup
1 stalk lemongrass
4 kaffir lime leaves
1 quart chicken stock
1 tablespoon Tom Yam, or other chili sauce
3 tablespoons fish sauce
2 tablespoons fresh lime juice

To Assemble
2 cups mixed sautéed vegetables, I prefer peas, carrots, mushrooms, and greens
Buckwheat noodles, cooked
Fresh cilantro, chopped

For the Chicken
Preheat the water bath to 141°F (60.5°C).

Salt and pepper the chicken and place in the sous vide bag. Seal the bag and cook the chicken for 2 to 4 hours, until pasteurized.

For the Hot and Sour Soup
Cut off the top of lemongrass, using only the bottom 4 to 5 inches and cut into large chunks. Cut or tear the kaffir lime leaves into strips.

Place the chicken stock, lemongrass, and kaffir lime leaves in a pot and bring to a simmer. Let the flavors infuse for at least 15 minutes, and up to 30 minutes. Strain the lemongrass and kaffir lime leaves out of the soup.

Stir in the Tom Yam sauce and fish sauce and bring to a boil. Remove from the heat. Right before serving stir in the lime and add additional lime juice, salt, or Tom Yam sauce to balance the soup.

To Assemble
Take the chicken breasts out of the water bath and remove them from the bag. Dry them off thoroughly using paper towels or a dish cloth. Quickly sear the chicken for 1 to 2 minutes per side, until just browned, then remove from the heat and cut into strips.

Place some of the sautéed vegetables in the bottom of a bowl and top with the buckwheat noodles. Add the sliced chicken and a ladle or two of the soup. Sprinkle the cilantro on top then serve.

Tortilla Soup with Shredded Pork

Cooks: 156°F (68.8°C) for 18 to 24 hours • Serves: 8
Nutritional: Cal 273; Fat 14g; Protein 19g; Carb 20g; Fiber 7g; Sugar 8g; Chol 43mg

My wife loves a rich and spicy tortilla soup so I've been working on a go-to recipe I can make for her. There's lots of ingredients, so it can look intimidating, but it is actually really easy to put together. The smell of the soup cooking on the stove will also fill your house with anticipation for dinner! This recipe makes a ton of soup, but it is real easy to freeze the leftovers for easy meals in a week or two.

Make sure you start the soup at least 30 to 45 minutes before you want to serve it because it is better when it lightly simmers for at least 20 minutes, or even as long as an hour or so. There are both chipotle pepper powder and jalapeños in this dish. You can always omit them, reduce the amount, or double the amount, depending on how spicy you like your food to be!

I also call for chicken stock, and it is best if you use a high-quality stock, preferably homemade. It adds so much more body and richness than a store-bought broth; plus it's much more nutritious. And lastly, you can always skip the sour cream, cheese, and tortillas at the end, the soup will still be fantastic without it!

For the Shredded Pork

1 pound pork shoulder (450 grams)
¼ teaspoon paprika, preferably smoked paprika
¼ teaspoon garlic powder
⅛ teaspoon ground coriander
⅛ teaspoon ground cumin
⅛ teaspoon chipotle pepper powder, or other chile powder
⅛ teaspoon ground cinnamon

For the Tortilla Soup

1 onion, diced
1 carrot, diced
½ green bell pepper, diced
½ red bell pepper, diced
1 jalapeño, diced
4 cloves garlic, coarsely chopped
6 tomatoes, diced, preferably paste tomatoes
6 cups chicken stock
2 tablespoons cornmeal, optional

To Assemble

2 avocados, peeled and sliced
4 corn tortillas, cut into thin strips, optional
Cheddar cheese, optional
1 to 2 jalapeño peppers, sliced
Fresh cilantro, chopped
Sour cream, optional
8 lime wedges

For the Shredded Pork

Preheat the water bath to 156°F (68.8°C).

If the pork shoulder is too large to fit into a bag, cut it into multiple pieces. Mix the spices together in a bowl then coat the pork with them. Place the pork in a sous vide bag then seal. Cook the pork for 18 to 24 hours.

For the Tortilla Soup

Heat some oil in a pot over medium heat. Add the onion, carrot, peppers, jalapeño and garlic to the oil and cook until softened. Add the tomatoes, chicken stock, and cornmeal. Bring to a simmer and let barely simmer uncovered for at least 20 minutes, and up to 60 minutes, for the vegetables to break down and the soup to reduce and thicken.

To Assemble

Take the pork shoulder out of the water bath and remove it from the bag. Dry it off thoroughly with a paper towel or dish cloth. Quickly sear the pork for 1 to 2 minutes per side, until just browned, then remove from the heat. Shred the pork with a fork and tongs then lightly salt it. You can add the pork juices to the tortilla soup for extra porky flavor.

Place a ladle or two of tortilla soup into a bowl. Add a handful of the shredded pork. Top with the avocados, tortilla strips, cheddar cheese, and jalapeño slices. Sprinkle with the cilantro, add a dollop of sour cream and serve with a lime wedge on the side.

Curried Butternut Squash Soup

Cooks: 183°F (83.9°C) for 1 to 4 hours • Serves: 4
Nutritional: Cal 214; Fat 11g; Protein 5g; Carb 28g; Fiber 6g; Sugar 12g; Chol 8mg

Making pureed soups is very easy to do with sous vide. Cooking the vegetables for between one and four hours allows them to break down fully, making it easy to simply add some liquid and puree them into a soup.

This version is a curried butternut squash but it works well with most winter squashes or, with slight variations, with many root vegetables. You can also add more or less curry paste, depending on how spicy you want it.

For the Butternut Squash
1 medium butternut squash, about 2 pounds (900 grams)
3 cloves garlic, coarsely chopped
1 tablespoon freshly grated ginger
2 teaspoons red curry paste
1 tablespoon butter or olive oil
Juice from ½ of a lime
½ cup vegetable broth or chicken stock
¼ cup coconut milk

To Assemble
2 shallots, sliced
Maple syrup
¼ cup roasted pumpkin seeds
1 lime
Fresh Thai basil leaves, or fresh Italian basil

For the Butternut Squash
Preheat a water bath to 183°F (83.9°C).

Peel the squash then cut in half and remove the seeds. Cut the flesh into ½" chunks (13mm). You should have about 2 cups.

Place the cubed squash in one or two sous vide bags, making sure it is in a single layer. Add the garlic, ginger, red curry paste, and butter to the sous vide bag. Seal the bag and cook for at least an hour, but preferably 2 to 4.

Once cooked, remove the squash from the sous vide bag and place in a blender or food processor. Add the lime juice, vegetable broth, coconut milk, salt and pepper then blend until fully pureed.

To Assemble
Sauté the shallots in a pan with olive oil until they brown and begin to get crispy. Remove from the heat and pat dry.

Place a ladle or two of the soup in a bowl then drizzle with maple syrup. Sprinkle with some roasted pumpkin seeds, top with the shallots, zest some lime over the soup and add a Thai basil leaf or two then serve.

Creamy Parsnip Soup

Cooks: 183°F (83.9°C) for 1 hour • Serves: 4 to 6
Nutritional: Cal 172; Fat 4g; Protein 6g; Carb 30g; Fiber 5g; Sugar 13g; Chol 5mg

I first had a version of this amazing winter soup when I was cooking from the book *A Boat, a Whale, and a Walrus*. The original version is super rich with lots of butter and cream and was a decadant meal for special occasions, but I wanted something I could eat more often without feeling guilty. The result is this much lighter version that still retains much of the creaminess of the original while using much less butter and cream. The soup will get smoother and smoother the more chicken stock you add, so you can tailor it to the texture you prefer. I love to serve it with some hearty whole grain bread you can use to sop up all the soup.

For the Parsnip Soup
- 1 leek, trimmed, washed, and tender end coarsely chopped
- 2 apples such as gala or honey crisp, peeled, cored, and coarsely chopped
- 1 pound parsnips, coarsely chopped (450 grams)
- 2 tablespoon butter or olive oil, optional
- 3 to 4 cups chicken stock or vegetable broth

To Assemble
- 4 spoonfuls heavy cream, optional
- Walnut oil or olive oil
- Nutmeg, preferably fresh but pre-ground will work
- Whole grain bread, optional

For the Parsnip Soup
Preheat a water bath to 183°F (83.9°C).

Place the leek, apples, parsnips and butter in one or two sous vide bags, making sure it is in a single layer. Lightly salt and pepper the mixture then seal the bag and cook for at least an hour.

Once cooked, remove the cooked mixture from the sous vide bag and place in a blender or food processor. Add the chicken stock then blend until smooth and fully pureed. Salt and pepper to taste.

To Assemble
Place a ladle or two of the soup into a bowl then swirl in a spoonful of the heavy cream. Drizzle with the walnut oil, grate some nutmeg on top, then serve.

Turkey and Avocado Salad

Cooks: 141°F (60.5°C) for 2 to 4 hours • Serves: 4
Nutritional: Cal 378; Fat 25g; Protein 31g; Carb 9g; Fiber 5g; Sugar 3g; Chol 70mg

Moist turkey with creamy avocado pairs with a bright lemon dressing and salty Parmesan cheese in this filling recipe. Sous vide turkey always turns out perfectly and the little bit of spice rub adds some nuanced background flavors to round out the dish.

For the Sous Vide Turkey
1 pound turkey breast (450 grams)
1 teaspoon ground coriander
½ teaspoon ground cumin
⅛ teaspoon chipotle pepper powder, or other chile powder

For the Lemon Vinaigrette
¼ cup olive oil
3 tablespoons fresh lemon juice

To Assemble
8 cups mixed greens
1 avocado, seed removed and flesh sliced
Fresh grated Parmesan cheese
1 lemon

For the Sous Vide Turkey
Preheat the water bath to 141°F (60.5°C).

Mix the spices together in a bowl. Salt and pepper the turkey and sprinkle with some of the spice mixture. Add to the sous vide bag, seal, and place in the water bath. Cook the turkey for 2 to 4 hours, until pasteurized.

For the Lemon Vinaigrette
Whisk or blend together all of the vinaigrette ingredients then salt and pepper to taste.

To Assemble
Take the turkey breasts out of the water bath and remove them from the bag. Dry them thoroughly with a paper towel or dish cloth. Quickly sear the turkey for 1 to 2 minutes per side, until just browned, then remove from the heat. Cut the turkey into strips.

Place the mixed greens on a plate and add the turkey. Fan the avocado slices out on top of the turkey. Drizzle the lemon vinaigrette on top then shave some Parmesan curls onto the salad using a vegetable peeler. Zest the lemon on top then serve.

Duck Breast Salad with Cherry Vinaigrette

Cooks: 131°F (55°C) for 2 to 3 hours • Serves: 4
Nutritional: Cal 402; Fat 28g; Protein 22g; Carb 21g; Fiber 5g; Sugar 14g; Chol 21mg

I always enjoy eating rich and fatty duck breast but sometimes I want to still have it be a light meal. Using it in a salad of mixed greens topped with a cherry vinaigrette is a wonderful way to enjoy the duck while still eating something that won't make you leave the table feeling heavy.

For the Duck Breast
2 duck breasts
1 teaspoon Chinese five-spice powder

For the Cherry Vinaigrette
15 cherries, pitted and halved
2 tablespoons balsamic vinegar
¼ cup olive oil

To Assemble
8 cups mixed greens
16 cherries, pitted and halved
½ cup walnuts, chopped
16 cherry tomatoes, halved
Fresh mint leaves, chopped

For the Duck Breast
Preheat a water bath to 131°F (55°C).

Lightly salt and pepper the duck breasts then sprinkle with the Chinese five-spice powder. Place in a sous vide bag then seal. Cook the duck breasts for 2 to 3 hours until heated through.

For the Cherry Vinaigrette
Place all the ingredients in a blender or food processor and process until smooth and creamy.

To Assemble
Remove the cooked duck from the sous vide bag and dry it off thoroughly using paper towels or a dish cloth. Lightly salt the duck breast then quickly sear it until the outside has browned and the fat has begun to render. Cut the duck into slices.

Place the mixed greens in a bowl and add the slices of duck. Top with the cherries, walnuts, and tomatoes then drizzle with the cherry vinaigrette. Top with the chopped mint leaves then serve.

Top Round Salad with Watercress and Kale

Cooks: 131°F (55°C) for 1 to 2 days • Serves: 4
Nutritional: Cal 452; Fat 30g; Protein 31g; Carb 18g; Fiber 5g; Sugar 5g; Chol 62mg

Top round is a very lean but tough piece of meat that really shines with sous vide. After 1 to 2 days it turns very tender. It is definitely a milder cut of meat, and can sometimes be on the dry side, so I like to pair it with a flavorful salad for a light summer meal. The peppery watercress combines with the earthy kale for a nuanced base salad that is brightened up with the lemon vinaigrette. Pomegranate seeds and berries add bursts of sweetness without overwhelming the taste of the steak.

For an upscale version of this salad, you can use filet mignon and just cook it until heated through, about 1 to 3 hours.

For the Top Round
1 pound top round (450 grams)
1 teaspoon ground coriander
½ teaspoon ground cumin
¼ teaspoon mustard powder

For the Lemon Shallot Vinaigrette
3 tablespoons fresh lemon juice
1 shallot, diced
¼ cup olive oil

To Assemble
1 ½ cups cleaned and chopped watercress
4 cups cleaned and chopped kale
5 radishes, sliced into half moons
1 cup blueberries
½ cup pecans
¼ cup roasted pumpkin seeds
¼ cup pomegranate seeds
Freshly cracked black pepper

For the Top Round
Preheat the water bath to 131°F (55°C).

Mix the spices together in a bowl. Salt and pepper the meat and sprinkle with some of the spice mixture. Add to the sous vide bag, seal, and place in the water bath. Cook the top round for 1 to 2 days.

For the Lemon Shallot Vinaigrette
Whisk or blend together all of the vinaigrette ingredients then salt and pepper to taste.

To Assemble
Take the top round out of the water bath and remove it from the bag. Dry it thoroughly with a paper towel or dish cloth. Quickly sear the top round for 1 to 2 minutes per side, until just browned, then remove from the heat and cut into strips.

Place the kale and watercress on a plate and drizzle with some of the lemon shallot vinaigrette. Toss lightly to mix. Top with the strips of top round, the radishes, blueberries, pecans, pumpkin seeds and pomegranate seeds. Drizzle with the remaining lemon shallot vinaigrette, crack fresh pepper over the top of the salad then serve.

Watermelon and Cucumber Salad with Cod

Cooks: 130°F (54.4°C) for 30 to 60 minutes • Serves: 4
Nutritional: Cal 306; Fat 16g; Protein 27g; Carb 15g; Fiber 2g; Sugar 10g; Chol 82mg

In summertime I love to cook with watermelons. They are so light and flavorful and can result in some really unique dishes. For this meal, I combine them with cucumbers, jalapeño, and lime for a sweet and spicy salad full of crunch.

I usually like to serve it with a light fish such as cod or tilapia so the watermelon still manages to shine.

For the Cod
1 pound of cod fillets (450 grams)
2 sprigs fresh rosemary

For the Watermelon and Cucumber Salad
3 cups diced watermelon
1 cucumber, diced
1 jalapeño pepper, diced
2 tablespoons fresh lime juice
2 tablespoons avocado oil, or olive oil
1 cup lightly packed arugula

To Assemble
1 cup crumbled feta cheese
½ cup chopped fresh cilantro
⅓ cup chopped fresh mint leaves
Zest from 2 limes

For the Cod
Preheat a water bath to 130°F (54.4°C).

Clean the cod and cut into portions if needed. Liberally salt and pepper the cod then place in a sous vide bag with the rosemary and seal. Let the cod sit for 30 minutes for the dry brine to take effect.

Place the bag in the water bath and cook the cod for 30 to 60 minutes, until heated through.

For the Watermelon and Cucumber Salad
Toss the watermelon, cucumber, and jalapeño with the lime juice and avocado oil. Salt and pepper it to taste then stir in the arugula.

To Assemble
Remove the cod from the bag and dry it off thoroughly using paper towels or a dish cloth. Briefly sear the cod on one side.

Put some of the salad onto a plate. Place the cod on the side of the salad and sprinkle everything with the feta, cilantro, mint, and lime zest, then serve.

Warm Peach and Blue Cheese Salad

Cooks: 165°F (73.8°C) for 20 to 40 minutes • Serves: 4
Nutritional: Cal 227; Fat 15g; Protein 7g; Carb 17g; Fiber 3g; Sugar 13g; Chol 13mg

Sometimes I am up for a light snack that will hold me over until dinner time. This mixture of peaches and blue cheese always does the trick. I was originally unsure of the flavor combinations but once I tried it together I was won over. This salad works best in the height of peach season, though sometimes I eat them all before I get around to actually cooking them!

For the Peaches
- 4 peaches, pits removed and cut in half
- ¼ teaspoon ground cinnamon
- 1 tablespoon Calvados or apple brandy

To Assemble
- ½ cup crumbled blue cheese
- Honey, optional
- ½ cup chopped walnuts
- ⅓ cup chopped fresh mint leaves

For the Peaches
Preheat a water bath to 165°F (73.8°C).

Sprinkle the peaches with the cinnamon. Place in a sous vide bag with the Calvados then lightly seal. Cook the peaches for 20 to 40 minutes, until heated through and tender.

To Assemble
Remove the peaches from the sous vide bag and place on a plate. Pour some of the juices over the top then sprinkle with the blue cheese. Drizzle with the honey, top with the walnut and mint then serve.

Tuna and Ginger Sesame Salad

Cooks: 110°F (43.3°C) for 20 to 60 minutes • Serves: 4
Nutritional: Cal 650; Fat 35g; Protein 52g; Carb 32g; Fiber 12g; Sugar 8g; Chol 67mg

Lightly seared tuna is one of those lunch meals that tastes great and fills me up without leaving me feeling heavy afterwards. Sometimes I have trouble making sure the middle is warm without overcooking the outside. Cooking it with sous vide at a lower temperature ensures it is heated throughout without over cooking it at all. Finishing it off with a really quick sear adds some color and texture while leaving the rest of the tuna perfectly done.

For the Tuna
- 2 large tuna steaks
- ¼ teaspoon ground cinnamon
- ¼ teaspoon ginger powder
- ⅛ teaspoon ground cloves
- ⅛ teaspoon cayenne pepper powder
- 2 tablespoons olive oil

For the Ginger-Soy Vinaigrette
- 2 tablespoons chopped ginger
- ¼ cup olive oil
- ¼ cup rice wine vinegar
- 3 tablespoons soy sauce
- 3 tablespoons sesame oil
- 1 tablespoon honey, optional

To Assemble
- 8 cups mixed greens, preferably with watercress or arugula
- 18 snow peas, cut into batons if desired
- 4 ounces shiitake mushrooms, sliced
- 4 radishes, sliced into half moons
- White and black sesame seeds

For the Tuna
Preheat a water bath to 110°F (43.3°C).

Mix together the spices in a small bowl. Lightly salt and pepper the tuna and sprinkle with some of the spice mixture. Then place in a sous vide bag, add the olive oil and seal. Cook until heated through, 20 to 60 minutes.

For the Ginger-Soy Vinaigrette
Place all the ingredients in a blender or food processor and process until smooth and creamy.

To Assemble
Gently remove the cooked tuna from the sous vide bag and dry it thoroughly using paper towels or a dish cloth. Lightly salt the tuna then very quickly sear it until the outside has browned. Cut it into slices.

Place the mixed greens on a plate and add the tuna. Top with the snow peas, mushrooms and radishes. Drizzle with the ginger-soy vinaigrette. Sprinkle with the sesame seeds then serve.

Grain Bowls

Nothing tastes better to me for lunch than a double cheeseburger with French fries...at least until I crash into a food coma 2 hours later.

When I want to keep my energy up all day, but still eat something hearty and filled with flavor, I've found grain bowls to be an amazing option. The combination of sweet vegetables, hearty grains, and some meat or fish, topped with a flavorful sauce makes for a filling lunch.

In this chapter I give you many of my favorite, go-to grain bowls. They have tons of flavor and each ingredient is designed to complement the others...but sometimes I'll just take whatever leftover grains, vegetables and meat I can find in my fridge, toss them into a bowl and chow down! So please feel free to mix and match the proteins, sauces, and grains in these recipes to create your own go-to combinations.

Note: In these recipes I recommend the time and temperatures I prefer, but for more options you can refer to the "Common Temperature Ranges" section at the start of the "Recipes" chapter or the "Cooking by Tenderness" chapter.

Simple Sous Vide Grains

Cooks: 183°F (83.9°C) for 20 to 60 minutes • Makes: 1 pint
Quinoa Nutritional: Cal 104; Fat 2g; Protein 4g; Carb 18g; Fiber 2g; Sugar 0g; Chol 0mg
Farro Nutritional: Cal 98; Fat 1g; Protein 4g; Carb 20g; Fiber 3g; Sugar 2g; Chol 0mg
Bulgur Nutritional: Cal 76; Fat 0g; Protein 3g; Carb 17g; Fiber 4g; Sugar 0g; Chol 0mg
Average Nutritional: Cal 93; Fat 1g; Protein 4g; Carb 18g; Fiber 3g; Sugar 1g; Chol 0mg

Most grains are convenient to cook with sous vide, both because it makes it easy to replicate your results but also for the lack of cleanup required. I usually cook the grains in 1-pint or 1-quart Mason jars, depending on how much I need. I'll often leave the grains in the jars, chill them in cold water, and refrigerate them for later use. You can also mix and match grains, as long as they get done at about the same time.

The cooking time will depend entirely on the type of grain, but in general, it takes about 20% longer than is called for on the stove. The amount of liquid needed is also dependent on the grain, but is usually about 80% of what you usually need due to the lack of evaporation. I have used the below recipe on quinoa, farro, bulgur wheat and several others with great success.

For the Sous Vide Grains
⅔ cup grains
1 ⅓ cups water
A dash of salt

For the Sous Vide Grains
Preheat a water bath to 183°F (83.9°C).

Combine the grains, water, and salt in a pint Mason jar. Hand tighten the lid, making sure not to over tighten it. Shake up the Mason jar then carefully place it in the water bath. Cook the grains for 20 to 60 minutes, until the water is absorbed and the grains are cooked through. Remove from the Mason jar and fluff with a fork before serving.

Halibut with Melon and Wheat Berries

Cooks: 130°F (54.4°C) for 30 to 60 minutes • Serves: 4
Nutritional: Cal 371; Fat 21g; Protein 24g; Carb 24g; Fiber 4g; Sugar 8g; Chol 69mg

With a relatively bold flavor, halibut pairs well with many things but for this summer salad I combine it with sweet cantaloupe, zesty feta, and sour lemon for a simple but tasty dish. The addition of wheat berries rounds it all out with a nutty and sweet flavor. This dish also works well with other white fish, or even chicken and turkey.

For the Halibut
1 pound of halibut fillets (450 grams)
1 sprig fresh rosemary

For the Melon and Feta Salad
2 cups diced cantaloupe
1 cup cooked wheat berries
½ cup crumbled feta cheese
2 tablespoons fresh lemon juice
¼ cup chopped fresh parsley
2 tablespoons chopped fresh mint leaves

To Assemble
1 lemon, zested

For the Halibut
Preheat a water bath to 130°F (54.4°C).

Clean the halibut and cut into portions if needed. Liberally salt and pepper the halibut then place in a sous vide bag with the rosemary and seal. Let the halibut sit for 30 minutes for the dry brine to take effect.

Cook the halibut for 30 to 60 minutes, until heated through.

For the Melon and Feta Salad
Toss all the ingredients together then salt and pepper to taste.

To Assemble
Remove the halibut from the bag and dry thoroughly using paper towels or a dish cloth. Briefly sear the halibut on one side.

Place the melon and feta salad on a plate and top with the halibut. Sprinkle with the lemon zest then serve.

Cuban Style Beef Bowl

Cooks: 131°F (55°C) for 12 to 24 hours • Serves: 4
Nutritional: Cal 815; Fat 29g; Protein 41g; Carb 109g; Fiber 18g; Sugar 27g; Chol 78mg

This is a filling grain bowl that pops with flavor. The rich and beefy skirt steak is cut by the sour mojo sauce, and the mango and plantains add bursts of sweetness. The spelt and black beans bulk it out. I love the all-natural sweetness added with the fried plantain and the mango, but you can omit them if you want to reduce the sugar in the recipe.

For the Skirt Steak
1 pound skirt steak (450 grams)
1 teaspoon ground cumin
½ teaspoon garlic powder
½ teaspoon dried oregano

For the Mojo Sauce
3 tablespoons olive oil
8 cloves garlic, minced
⅓ cup fresh orange juice
⅓ cup fresh lime juice
1 teaspoon ground cumin
2 tablespoons chopped fresh oregano leaves

For the Fried Plantain
1 plantain, peeled and thickly sliced

To Assemble
2 cups cooked spelt
1 cup cooked black beans
1 mango, diced
½ red onion, diced
¼ cup chopped fresh oregano leaves
4 lime wedges

For the Skirt Steak
Preheat a water bath to 131°F (55°C).

Mix together the spices in a bowl. Lightly salt and pepper the skirt steak then sprinkle with the spices. Place in a sous vide bag then seal. Cook the skirt steak for 12 to 24 hours until tenderized.

For the Mojo Sauce
To prepare the mojo sauce heat the olive oil and garlic in a pan over medium-high heat. Cook until the garlic begins to soften, about 2 minutes after it starts to sizzle. Add the orange juice, lime juice and cumin then bring to a simmer. Stir in the oregano and remove from the heat.

For the Fried Plantain
Heat some oil in a pan over medium-high heat. Add the plantain slices in a single layer and cook until they start to brown, flip them and repeat until tender.

To Assemble
Remove the cooked skirt steak from the sous vide bag and dry thoroughly using paper towels or a dish cloth. Lightly salt the skirt steak then quickly sear it for 1 to 2 minutes per side, until just browned. Cut the skirt steak into slices.

Place the spelt in a bowl then add the black beans and fried plantains. Add the skirt steak and top with the mango and red onion. Drizzle with the mojo sauce, sprinkle with the oregano, add a lime wedge to the side then serve.

Chicken and Avocado Bowl

Cooks: 141°F (60.5°C) for 2 to 4 hours • Serves: 4
Nutritional: Cal 462; Fat 20g; Protein 34g; Carb 41g; Fiber 13g; Sugar 7g; Chol 83mg

This is a super simple recipe to toss together when you need a filling but quick meal. The lemon helps to brighten up the dish while the radishes and cucumber intrroduce a pleasant crunch. The lemon and olive oil add brightness to the dish without overwhelming it. This recipe works equally well with turkey breast.

For the Sous Vide Chicken
2 chicken breasts
4 slices of lemon

To Assemble
1 cup cooked millet
1 cup cooked red quinoa
4 radishes, sliced
1 cucumber, diced
Arugula or other greens
2 avocados, peeled and flesh sliced
Olive oil
¼ cup pomegranate seeds
¼ cup chopped fresh basil leaves
8 lemon wedges

For the Sous Vide Chicken
Preheat the water bath to 141°F (60.5°C).

Salt and pepper the chicken and place in the sous vide bag. Place 2 slices of lemon on each then seal the bag. Cook the chicken for 2 to 4 hours, until pasteurized.

To Assemble
Remove the cooked chicken from the sous vide bag and dry thoroughly using paper towels or a dish cloth. Lightly salt the chicken then quickly sear it for 1 to 2 minutes per side, until just browned. Remove from the heat and cut the chicken into strips.

Place the grains into a bowl and top with the radishes, cucumber, and arugula. Add the chicken then fan the avocado out on top of it. Drizzle with some olive oil then sprinkle with the pomegranate seeds and basil. Add 2 lemon wedges to the side, then serve.

Duck and Roasted Vegetable Bowl

Cooks: 131°F (55°C) for 2 to 3 hours • Serves: 4
Nutritional: Cal 484; Fat 16g; Protein 28g; Carb 63g; Fiber 10g; Sugar 17g; Chol 64mg

This is a hearty but nutritious meal featuring rich duck, flavorful roasted vegetables and nutty farro, all topped off with a light mixture of orange juice and soy sauce. It's a meal I love to eat when the temperature starts dropping in fall, it warms me up and gets me ready to face the second half of the day.

For the Duck Breast
2 duck breasts
2 teaspoons garlic powder
½ teaspoon ginger powder
¼ teaspoon ground cloves
4 sprigs fresh thyme

For the Roasted Vegetables
2 pints mixed mushrooms, cleaned and destemmed
2 sweet potatoes, diced
2 sweet onions, sliced
2 turnips, diced

For the Orange Soy Sauce
⅓ cup fresh orange juice
3 tablespoons olive oil
1 tablespoon soy sauce

To Assemble
2 cups cooked farro
¼ cup chopped fresh parsley

For the Duck Breast
Preheat a water bath to 131°F (55°C).

Mix together the spices in a bowl. Lightly salt and pepper the duck breasts then sprinkle with the spices. Place in a sous vide bag with the thyme then seal. Cook the duck breasts for 2 to 3 hours until heated through.

For the Roasted Vegetables
Preheat an oven to 400°F (200°C).

Working with each type of vegetable separately, toss with olive oil then salt and pepper them. Place on a roasting sheet then cook, stirring once or twice, about 30 to 60 minutes or until tender, removing each type of vegetable separately once it is done.

For the Orange Soy Sauce
Whisk all the ingredients together.

To Assemble
Remove the cooked duck from the sous vide bag and dry thoroughly using paper towels or a dish cloth. Lightly salt the duck breast then quickly sear it until the outside has browned and the fat has begun to render. Cut the duck into slices.

Place the farro in a bowl and surround with the roasted vegetables. Top with the duck breast and drizzle with the sauce. Sprinkle with the parsley then serve.

Shrimp and Quinoa Bowl

Cooks: 130°F (54.4°C) for 15 to 35 minutes • Serves: 4
Nutritional: Cal 483; Fat 23g; Protein 34g; Carb 40g; Fiber 6g; Sugar 9g; Chol 191mg

Shrimp cooked sous vide is always plump and juicy, with none of the rubberiness you can find in the pan fried version. Here I combine it with a hearty quinoa salad filled with spinach, black beans and roasted red peppers, all topped off with tangy feta cheese!

There are several temperatures you can use to cook shrimp, but for "normal" shrimp I prefer 130°F (54.4°C). Some people like it cooked lower, down to 122°F (50°C) and others like it a little tougher at 140°F (60°C). Experiment with the different temperatures and see what works best for you!

For the Shrimp
1 pound shrimp, peeled and cleaned (450 grams)
½ teaspoon sweet paprika
½ teaspoon garlic powder

For the Vinaigrette
3 tablespoons white wine vinegar
2 tablespoons orange juice
1 tablespoon honey
1 shallot, diced
5 tablespoons olive oil

To Assemble
2 cups cooked quinoa
1 cup baby spinach leaves
½ cup cooked corn kernels
½ cup cooked black beans
¼ cup diced roasted red peppers
¼ red onion, diced
½ cucumber, diced
¼ cup crumbled feta cheese

For the Shrimp
Preheat a water bath to 130°F (54.4°C).

Place the shrimp in a sous vide bag in a single layer. Seal the bag then cook for 15 to 35 minutes, until heated through.

For the Vinaigrette
Whisk together the vinegar, orange juice, and honey. Stir in the shallot and let sit for 10 minutes. Slowly whisk in the olive oil until fully emulsified. Salt and pepper to taste.

To Assemble
Combine all the ingredients in a bowl then divvy up into individual bowls. Remove the shrimp from the bag and add to the bowls. Drizzle the vinaigrette over the top and serve.

Pork and Ginger Bowl

Cooks: 140°F (60°C) for 2 to 3 hours • Serves: 4
Nutritional: Cal 488; Fat 19g; Protein 34g; Carb 49g; Fiber 5g; Sugar 13g; Chol 71mg

Using an easy to make but super flavorful ginger sauce is a really effective way to add depth to a grain bowl. It's a combination of many Asian ingredients all blended together, with the ginger being the star of the show. Topping the bowl with moist sous vide pork, baby corn, carrots and steamed collard greens rounds out the meal.

For the Pork Chops
1 pound pork chops (450 grams)
½ teaspoon garlic powder
½ teaspoon ground coriander
¼ teaspoon ground cumin
⅛ teaspoon ground cinnamon
1/16 teaspoon ground cloves

For the Ginger Sauce
3 tablespoons olive oil
3 tablespoons soy sauce
2 tablespoons minced ginger
1 tablespoon fish sauce
2 tablespoons honey
1 tablespoon rice wine vinegar
2 teaspoons sesame oil
2 cloves garlic, roughly chopped
⅛ teaspoon cayenne pepper powder, or red pepper flakes

To Assemble
1 cup cooked rye
1 cup cooked freekeh
16 baby corns
16 carrot sticks
2 cups steamed or sautéed collard greens
¼ cup sprouts, preferably sunflower if available

For the Pork Chops
Preheat a water bath to 140°F (60°C).

Mix together the spices in a bowl. Lightly salt and pepper the pork chop then sprinkle with the spices. Place in a sous vide bag then seal the bag and cook for 2 to 3 hours, until heated through or pasteurized.

For the Ginger Sauce
Place all the ingredients in a blender or food processor and process until smooth. Salt and pepper to taste.

To Assemble
Remove the cooked pork chops from the sous vide bag and dry thoroughly using paper towels or a dish cloth. Lightly salt the pork then quickly sear it for 1 to 2 minutes per side, until just browned, then remove from the heat. Cut the pork into bite-sized pieces if desired.

Place the rye and freekeh in a bowl and top with the pork. Add the baby corn, carrot sticks, and collard greens. Drizzle with the ginger sauce, top with the sprouts, then serve.

Garlic and Parsley Lamb Chop Bowl

Cooks: 131°F (55°C) for 2 to 3 hours • Serves: 4
Nutritional: Cal 651; Fat 41g; Protein 34g; Carb 43g; Fiber 11g; Sugar 12g; Chol 85mg

Rich and meaty lamb chops pair wonderfully with a garlic, parsley and mint-based sauce. It keeps the dish light and highlights the flavor of the lamb. Adding grilled vegetables introduces more flavor and texture to the dish while the combination of quinoa and bulgur wheat makes it hearty.

For the Lamb Chop
- 1 pound lamb chops (450 grams)
- 1 teaspoon garlic powder
- ½ teaspoon paprika
- 2 sprigs fresh rosemary
- 2 sprigs fresh thyme leaves

For the Garlic-Parsley Sauce
- 2 cups lightly packed chopped fresh parsley
- 10 to 15 fresh mint leaves
- 2 cloves garlic, coarsely chopped
- ½ cup olive oil
- ½ cup water
- ¼ cup freshly grated Parmesan cheese
- 2 tablespoons fresh lemon juice

For the Grilled Vegetables
- 2 zucchini
- 2 red bell peppers
- 2 orange bell peppers
- 2 sweet onions
- 1 pound snap peas (450 grams)

To Assemble
- 1 cup cooked quinoa
- 1 cup cooked bulgur wheat
- ¼ cup chopped fresh basil leaves
- 12 nasturtium blossoms, optional

For the Lamb Chop
Preheat a water bath to 131°F (55°C).

Mix together the dried spices in a bowl. Lightly salt and pepper the lamb chops then sprinkle with the spices. Place in a sous vide bag with the rosemary and thyme then seal the bag. Cook for 2 to 3 hours, until heated through.

For the Garlic-Parsley Sauce
Place all the ingredients in a blender or food processor and process until smooth. Salt and pepper to taste.

For the Grilled Vegetables
Remove the stem from the zucchinis and cut in half length-wise. Remove the stem and seeds of the peppers then cut into whole sides. Toss the zucchini and peppers with olive oil then salt and pepper them.

Cut the onions into slabs, trying to keep the rings from separating for easy grilling. Brush with olive oil then salt and pepper them.

Toss the snap peas with olive oil then salt and pepper them.

Cook all the vegetables on the grill, or under a broiler, until they have taken on color and become tender. Remove from the heat and cut the zucchini, peppers, and onions into strips.

To Assemble
Remove the cooked lamb chops from the sous vide bag and dry thoroughly using paper towels or a dish cloth. Lightly salt the lamb then quickly sear it until it starts to brown.

Place the quinoa and bulgur in a bowl along with the grilled vegetables. Drizzle with the garlic-parsley sauce and top with the lamb chops. Sprinkle with basil leaves and nasturtium blossoms then serve.

Tuna Poke Bowl

Cooks: 110°F (43.3°C) for 20 to 40 minutes • Serves: 4
Nutritional: Cal 480; Fat 26g; Protein 25g; Carb 44g; Fiber 15g; Sugar 8g; Chol 22mg

Poke bowls are becoming more and more popular and showing up in restaurants around the country. The combination of fresh fish, an acidic dressing, and crisp vegetables is always satisfying. Many poke bowls are served cold, but I think heating the tuna in a low temperature bath allows more of the flavor to come through when you eat it. It also firms up the fish some as well. Be sure to use high quality tuna because you are still eating it raw. This also works well with salmon or other common sushi fish. Feel free to mix up the toppings or grains to anything you have on hand.

For the Tuna
½ pound yellowfin tuna, diced (225 grams)

For the Dressing
¼ cup soy sauce
2 tablespoons sesame oil
2 tablespoons fresh lime juice
1 tablespoon fresh lemon juice
1 teaspoon sriracha sauce

To Assemble
1 cup cooked wheat berries
1 cup cooked bulgur wheat
2 avocados, diced
¼ red onion, thinly sliced
1 cucumber, diced
1 scallion, thinly sliced
Sesame seeds

For the Tuna
Preheat a water bath to 110°F (43.3°C).

Liberally salt and pepper the tuna then place in a sous vide bag and seal. Let the tuna sit for 30 minutes for the dry brine to take effect. Cook the tuna for 20 to 40 minutes, until heated through.

For the Dressing
Whisk all the ingredients together then salt and pepper to taste.

To Assemble
Remove the tuna from the bag.

Place the wheat berries and bulgur in a bowl. Top with the tuna, avocados, red onion, and cucumber. Drizzle the dressing over the top. Sprinkle with the scallions and sesame seeds then serve.

Harissa Marinated Tofu and Kale Bowl

Cooks: 180°F (82.2°C) for 2 to 3 hours • Serves: 4
Nutritional: Cal 321; Fat 11g; Protein 20g; Carb 41g; Fiber 9g; Sugar 3g; Chol 0mg

It is safe to say that tofu isn't a favorite food of mine, but my father-in-law loves it and I wanted to try something special for him so I came up with this spicy tofu and kale bowl. Thanks to the Anova website I found a few variations on sous vide tofu recipes and adapted them to come up with this version.

Harissa is a spicy Moroccan red pepper sauce that is an easy way to spice up a dish, but if you can't find it you can substitute with any chile-sauce like sriracha or Huy Fong Chili Garlic Sauce.

When you seal the tofu in the sous vide bag, don't seal it on hard power or the tofu can be crushed. Either use the water displacement method or manually shut off your sealer once most of the air is out.

For the Tofu
- 1 package firm or extra-firm tofu, about 14 ounces (400 grams)
- 3 tablespoons harissa or other chile-garlic sauce
- 1 tablespoon soy sauce

For the Kale
- 1 tablespoon sesame oil
- 3 cups coarsely chopped kale
- 3 cloves garlic, minced
- 2 tablespoons minced ginger
- 2 tablespoons soy sauce
- 1 tablespoon rice wine vinegar

To Assemble
- 1 cup cooked farro
- 1 ½ cups cooked lentils
- ½ cup roasted red peppers
- ¼ cup chopped fresh basil leaves

For the Tofu
Preheat a water bath to 180°F (82.2°C).

Drain the tofu and cut into slabs ¾" to 1" thick (19mm to 25mm). Place the slabs on paper towels, top with more paper towels and a sheet pan lightly weighted down. Let sit for 20 to 30 minutes.

Mix the harissa and soy sauce together. Remove the sheet pan from the tofu and brush the tofu with the harissa mixture. Place the tofu in a sous vide bag then lightly seal the bag and cook for 2 to 3 hours.

For the Kale
Heat the sesame oil in a pan over medium heat. Add the kale, garlic, ginger, soy sauce and vinegar then cover and let cook until the kale is tender, about 10 to 20 minutes.

To Assemble
Remove the cooked tofu from the sous vide bag and dry thoroughly using paper towels or a dish cloth. Sear the tofu with a torch or under a broiler until it starts to brown. Remove from the heat and cut into bite-sized chunks.

Place the farro and lentils in a bowl and top with the kale and its juices. Add the tofu and the roasted red peppers. Sprinkle with the basil then serve.

Main Dish Meats

Ahhh, meat...my favorite!

I know some people give up certain types of meat when they are trying to eat healthier, but I just love it too much. My compromise has been to try and reduce the portions of meat I'm eating, while increasing the portion of vegetables.

I also tend to shy away from potatoes, fried vegetables, and other heavier sides. To boost the taste of the various dishes, I've also been utilizing more flavorful sauces that really tie the food together.

Below are some of the dishes I keep turning back to, many include meat, a side or two, and a sauce. You should feel comfortable if you want to substitute any of those components, or pick and choose among multiple recipes. There's no reason you can't serve the sauce from a steak with some pork, or replace the bison with beef! Or even if you've given up meat completely, you can use them with fish or vegetables.

> **Note:** In these recipes I recommend the time and temperatures I prefer, but for more options you can refer to the "Common Temperature Ranges" section at the start of the "Recipes" chapter or the "Cooking by Tenderness" chapter.

Filet Mignon with Roasted Brussels Sprouts

Cooks: 131°F (55°C) for 2 to 4 hours • Serves: 4
Nutritional: Cal 445; Fat 22g; Protein 35g; Carb 34g; Fiber 11g; Sugar 11g; Chol 73mg

Filet is a tender and very lean cut, making it a good choice for people trying to reduce their fat intake. I'll often cook a small tenderloin and serve it family style, with a big pile of Brussels sprouts. This allows everyone to select what they like best, but if you want to cut it up and serve it individually that works awesome as well!

For the Filet Mignon Steak

1 to 2 pounds filet mignon steaks or tenderloin roast (450 to 900 grams)

1 teaspoon garlic powder

½ teaspoon ground coriander

½ teaspoon ground cumin

3 sprigs fresh thyme

For the Roasted Brussels Sprouts

2 pounds Brussels sprouts (900 grams)

4 cloves garlic, minced

1 pint cherry tomatoes

For the Sautéed Onions

3 yellow onions, sliced

2 cloves garlic, minced

1 tablespoon white wine vinegar

To Assemble

1 tablespoon fresh lemon juice

2 tablespoons fresh thyme leaves

For the Filet Mignon Steak

Preheat the water bath to 131°F (55°C).

Mix the spices together in a bowl. Salt and pepper the steak and sprinkle with some of the spice mixture. Add to the sous vide bag with the thyme, seal, and place in the water bath. Cook the steak for 2 to 4 hours, until heated through.

For the Roasted Brussels Sprouts

Preheat an oven to 400°F (200°C).

Cut the ends off the Brussels sprouts and discard the ends. Cut the remaining portion in half lengthwise. Toss the Brussels sprouts and garlic in olive oil then salt and pepper them. Place on a roasting sheet then cook, stirring once or twice, until tender, about 30 to 45 minutes.

During the last 5 or 10 minutes, add the cherry tomatoes to the roasting sheet and cook until they just start to burst.

For the Sautéed Onions

Heat some oil in a pan over medium heat. Add the onions and garlic then cook until the onions become tender and start to lightly brown, about 15 to 20 minutes. Add the white wine vinegar and stir to mix well.

To Assemble

Take the steak out of the water bath and remove it from the bag. Dry it off thoroughly using paper towels or a dish cloth. Quickly sear the filet mignon for 1 to 2 minutes per side, until just browned, then remove from the heat.

Place the roasted Brussels sprouts and tomatoes in a bowl and drizzle with the fresh lemon juice. Add the steak and top with the sautéed onions. Sprinkle with the thyme leaves then serve.

Strip Steak with Roasted Cauliflower Puree

Cooks: 131°F (55°C) for 2 to 4 hours • Serves: 4
Nutritional: Cal 338; Fat 18g; Protein 31g; Carb 17g; Fiber 5g; Sugar 7g; Chol 63mg

I was raised on steak and potatoes, and I still love to sit down with a giant New York strip steak, a loaded baked potato and some macaroni and cheese...unfortunately, I also need to fit into my pants sometimes!

This meal is a nice compromise, it allows me to get my steak fix while replacing the sides with much lighter, but still tasty, options. The roasted cauliflower puree adds subtle flavors and some much needed lightness to the rich beef while the kale contributes some earthy base flavors.

For the Strip Steak

1 to 2 pounds strip steak (450 to 900 grams)
1 teaspoon ground coriander
½ teaspoon ground cumin
⅛ teaspoon chipotle pepper powder, or other chile powder

For the Roasted Cauliflower Puree

1 head of cauliflower, coarsely chopped
5 cloves garlic, coarsely chopped
2 shallots, minced
¼ cup chicken stock
1 tablespoon fresh lemon juice

For the Garlic Kale

1 bunch kale, washed and chopped
5 cloves garlic, minced
1 tablespoon minced ginger
1 tablespoon sherry vinegar

To Assemble

Paprika, preferably smoked paprika
12 cherry tomatoes, halved
1 roasted yellow bell pepper, diced
2 tablespoons fresh thyme leaves
Sea salt

For the Strip Steak

Preheat the water bath to 131°F (55°C).

Mix the spices together in a bowl. Salt and pepper the steak and sprinkle with some of the spice mixture. Add to the sous vide bag, seal, and place in the water bath. Cook the steak for 2 to 4 hours, until heated through.

For the Roasted Cauliflower Puree

Preheat an oven to 400°F (200°C).

Toss the cauliflower, garlic, and shallots in olive oil then salt and pepper it. Place on a roasting sheet then cook, stirring once or twice, about 20 to 30 minutes or until tender.

Place the roasted vegetables, chicken stock, and lemon juice in a blender or food processor and process until smooth.

For the Garlic Kale

Heat some oil in a pan over medium heat. Add the kale, garlic, ginger, and vinegar then cover and let cook until the kale is tender, about 10 to 20 minutes, stirring occasionally and adding small amounts of water as needed.

To Assemble

Take the strip steak out of the water bath and remove it from the bag. Dry it off thoroughly using paper towels or a dish cloth. Quickly sear the steak for 1 to 2 minutes per side, until just browned, then remove from the heat and cut it into serving sections.

Place the kale on a plate and top with the steak. Place a dollop of roasted cauliflower puree next to it and sprinkle the puree with the paprika. Place the tomatoes and peppers around the steak. Sprinkle with the thyme leaves and sea salt then serve.

Succotash with Hanger Steak

Cooks: 131°F (55°C) for 2 to 4 hours • Serves: 4
Nutritional: Cal 703; Fat 17g; Protein 61g; Carb 82g; Fiber 24g; Sugar 11g; Chol 105mg

Succotash is a classic, old school side mainly utilizing corn and lima beans with some poblano pepper added for heat and lime juice for acidity. It comes together very easily and is a great example of how simple a meal can be to make, especially when you use a tender cut of beef.

Unless you are pasteurizing them, the steak only needs to be heated through because the cut is already very tender. For most cuts this will be 2 to 4 hours, depending on the thickness. You can refer to the Cooking by Thickness chapter for specifics, though going an hour or so longer will not adversely affect the meat.

In this recipe you can also use cuts of medium toughness such as sirloin or flank steak, though since they are a little tougher you can increase the time they cook for a more tender steak.

For the Hanger Steak
1 ½ pounds hanger steak (680 grams)
¼ teaspoon steak seasoning or chile powder

For the Succotash
1 red onion, diced
2 cloves garlic, minced
1 poblano pepper, diced
2 cups corn kernels
2 cups lima beans
1 lime

To Assemble
¼ cup chopped fresh basil leaves

For the Hanger Steak
Preheat a water bath to 131°F (55°C).

Lightly salt the hanger steak then sprinkle with the steak seasoning. Place the steak in a sous vide bag then seal the bag and cook for 2 to 4 hours.

For the Succotash
Heat some olive oil in a pan over medium-high heat. Place the red onion in the pan and cook until it starts to soften. Add the garlic and poblano pepper and cook until the poblano pepper is tender. Add the corn and lima beans and cook until the lima beans are tender. Add some more olive oil then juice the lime in the pan and mix well to combine.

To Assemble
Remove the cooked steak from the bag and dry it off thoroughly using paper towels or a dish cloth. Quickly sear the steak for 1 to 2 minutes per side, until just browned, then remove from the heat and cut into serving sections.

Place a few spoonfuls of succotash on a plate then top with the steak. Sprinkle some basil on top and then lightly salt.

Shredded Beef with Yam Neua Sauce

Cooks: 165°F (73.9°C) for 18 to 24 hours • Serves: 4 to 6
Nutritional: Cal 326; Fat 20g; Protein 24g; Carb 14g; Fiber 2g; Sugar 8g; Chol 67mg

Yam neua is a Thai beef salad with a very memorable sauce of chile peppers, lime juice, shallots and fish sauce. It's filled with classic bold Thai flavors that burst in your mouth. I take that sauce and toss it with shredded beef, crisp veggies, and lots of fresh herbs.

I like the beef to have a shreddable texture, but if you prefer it more steak like you can decrease the temperature to 131°F (55°C) and increase the cooking time to 36 to 60 hours.

For the Shredded Beef
- 1 to 2 pounds chuck roast (450 to 900 grams)
- 1 teaspoon ancho pepper powder
- ½ teaspoon garlic powder
- ½ teaspoon onion powder

For the Yam Neua Sauce
- 2 shallots, sliced
- ½ Thai bird chile or serrano chile, diced
- Juice from 2 limes
- 1 teaspoon sugar
- 2 teaspoons maple syrup
- 2 tablespoons fish sauce
- 2 tablespoons olive oil

To Assemble
- ½ cucumber sliced
- 1 large carrot, peeled and cut into thin half moons
- 2 cups halved cherry tomatoes
- ½ cup coarsely chopped fresh cilantro
- ½ cup coarsely chopped fresh basil leaves
- ¼ cup coarsely chopped fresh mint leaves

For the Shredded Beef
Preheat a water bath to 165°F (73.9°C).

Mix together the spices in a bowl. Lightly salt and pepper the chuck roast then sprinkle with the spices. Add the chuck to the sous vide bag then seal. Place the bag in the water bath and cook for 18 to 24 hours.

For the Yam Neua Sauce
Combine the shallots, diced chiles, lime juice, sugar, maple syrup, and fish sauce in a bowl. Salt and pepper to taste then let sit 5 minutes. Whisk in the olive oil.

To Assemble
Salt the cucumber slices then let sit in a colander for 10 to 15 minutes to drain.

Take the beef out of the water bath and remove it from the bag. Dry it off thoroughly using paper towels or a dish cloth. Quickly sear the chuck for 1 to 2 minutes per side, until just browned, then remove from the heat and lightly shred the meat.

Place the shredded meat, cucumber, carrots, cherry tomatoes, cilantro, basil, and mint in a bowl then mix until thoroughly combined. Spoon out onto a plate then serve.

Chuck Steak with Asparagus and Shishito Peppers

Cooks: 131°F (55°C) for 36 to 60 hours • Serves: 4
Nutritional: Cal 427; Fat 23g; Protein 50g; Carb 7g; Fiber 2g; Sugar 3g; Chol 150mg

I love chuck steaks, but to offset the fattiness they have I try to pair them with really light sides. This recipe uses sautéed asparagus and cherry tomatoes, along with shishito peppers to fill out the meal and keep it from getting too heavy.

For the Chuck Steak
2 pounds chuck steak or chuck roast (900 grams)
1 teaspoon garlic powder
1 teaspoon onion powder
½ teaspoon ground coriander

For the Asparagus
1 bunch asparagus
1 pint cherry tomatoes
2 teaspoons diced garlic

To Assemble
4 shishito peppers
¼ cup coarsely chopped fresh sage
Sea salt

For the Chuck Steak
Preheat a water bath to 131°F (55°C).

If the chuck is large, cut it into 1 ½" to 2" slabs (38mm to 50mm) then trim off any excess fat or connective tissue.

Combine all the spices in a bowl and mix well. Lightly coat the chuck slabs with the spices then place in a sous vide bag. Seal the bag and cook for 36 to 60 hours.

For the Asparagus
Trim the bottom off of the asparagus and cut the cherry tomatoes in half.

Heat some olive oil in a pan over medium heat. Place the asparagus and garlic in the pan and cook until the asparagus becomes tender. Add the cherry tomatoes then remove the vegetables from the heat.

To Assemble
In a hot pan, sear the shishito peppers until they just start to brown, turning until all sides get color and they begin to become tender.

Remove the cooked steak from the bag and dry it off thoroughly with paper towels or a dish cloth. Salt the chuck and then quickly sear it for 1 to 2 minutes per side, until just browned, then remove from the heat. Cut the chuck into serving-sized portions.

Place a few spoonfuls of the asparagus and tomato mixture on a plate then top with the steak. Sprinkle some sage and sea salt over the dish then top with a seared shishito pepper.

Bison Strip Steak Carbonara

Cooks: 131°F (55°C) for 2 to 4 hours • Serves: 4
Nutritional: Cal 401; Fat 17g; Protein 50g; Carb 12g; Fiber 4g; Sugar 5g; Chol 107mg

This recipe showcases cooking other types of red meat. I focus on bison but it would work equally well with other tender cuts of red meat such as deer or elk. Bison is becoming more and more common but is still a pretty under-utilized cut of meat. Like steak, I prefer bison cooked to 131°F (55°C) but the temperature ranges for it are similar to beef so you can adjust how you see fit.

This recipe combines the bison with a semi-traditional egg-based carbonara sauce that I bulked up with some fresh vegetables. The richness of the carbonara helps to offset some of the leanness of the bison.

For the Bison Strip Steak
1 ½ to 2 pounds bison strip steak (700 to 900 grams)
1 sprig fresh rosemary
3 sprigs fresh thyme

For the Sautéed Vegetables
1 medium yellow onion, diced
1 yellow bell pepper, diced
1 red bell pepper, diced
1 small head of broccoli, cut into florets

To Assemble
4 cups cooked pasta, preferably whole wheat or rye-based
4 eggs
Freshly grated Parmesan cheese
⅓ cup coarsely chopped fresh basil leaves

For the Bison Strip Steak
Preheat a water bath to 131°F (55°C).

Lightly salt the bison then place it in a sous vide bag with the rosemary and thyme. Seal the bag and cook for 2 to 4 hours.

For the Sautéed Vegetables
Heat some oil over medium heat. Add the onion and cook until it begins to soften and turn translucent. Add the yellow and red bell peppers as well as the broccoli and cook until the broccoli is tender. Remove from the heat.

To Assemble
Remove the cooked bison from the bag, discarding the herbs, and dry it off thoroughly using paper towels or a dish cloth. Quickly sear the bison for 1 to 2 minutes per side, until just browned, then remove from the heat and cut into ½" slices (25mm).

Cook the pasta until done then immediately add to individual bowls and crack an egg into each one. Stir well to ensure the egg cooks in the pasta. Grate fresh Parmesan cheese into each bowl and stir well. Top with the sautéed vegetables, slices of bison, and basil. Grate some more cheese on top then serve.

Pork Chops with Broccolini and Roasted Peppers

Cooks: 140°F (60°C) for 2 to 3 hours • Serves: 4
Nutritional: Cal 478; Fat 16g; Protein 55g; Carb 31g; Fiber 10g; Sugar 8g; Chol 125mg

Traditionally cooked pork chops can be dry and tough, but using sous vide ensures they are moist and tender. I like to cook them and serve them with simple sides of vegetables. This recipe uses sautéed broccolini and roasted peppers to round it out.

For the Pork Chop
4 pork chops, preferably thick cut
1 teaspoon garlic powder
1 teaspoon onion powder
½ teaspoon ground coriander
4 sprigs fresh thyme

For the Broccolini
2 teaspoons diced garlic
2 bunches broccolini

For the Roasted Peppers
2 red bell peppers
2 yellow bell peppers

To Assemble
Sea salt

For the Pork Chop
Preheat a water bath to 140°F (60°C).

Mix together the spices in a bowl. Lightly salt and pepper the pork chops then sprinkle with the spices. Place in a sous vide bag with the thyme sprigs, then seal the bag and cook for 2 to 3 hours, until heated through or pasteurized.

For the Broccolini
Heat some olive oil in a pan over medium heat. Add the broccolini and garlic to the pan and cook until tender.

For the Roasted Peppers
Remove the stem and seeds of the peppers then cut into whole sides. Toss the peppers with olive oil then salt and pepper them. Cook under a broiler, or in a hot pan, until they have taken on color and become tender.

To Assemble
Remove the cooked pork chops from the bag and dry off thoroughly using paper towels or a dish cloth. Quickly sear the pork for 1 to 2 minutes per side, until just browned, then remove from the heat.

Place the pork chop on a plate and surround with the bell peppers. Top with the broccolini then drizzle with olive oil and sprinkle with sea salt.

Moroccan-Style Tajine with Pork Chops

Cooks: 140°F (60°C) for 2 to 3 hours • Serves: 4
Nutritional: Cal 579; Fat 19g; Protein 47g; Carb 62g; Fiber 11g; Sugar 17g; Chol 107mg

I love the complex flavors of tajines, with their sweet highs and nuanced undertones from the spices. One of the best I've made at home is from the *Moroccan Modern* cookbook, and I've come up with my own version that uses sous vide to perfectly cook the meat.

I like to serve this dish over some grains like farro and quinoa, or some cauliflower rice. The honey in this recipe isn't marked as optional but if you really are trying to reduce your sugar intake you can use less or leave it out, but the flavor balance will be affected.

For the Pork Chops
4 pork chops
1 teaspoon paprika
½ teaspoon ground ginger
½ teaspoon ground cumin
¼ teaspoon ground cloves
¼ teaspoon ground cinnamon
1 bay leaf, finely crumbled

For the Tajine
2 yellow onions, sliced
Juice of two oranges
1 cup water
2 tablespoons sweet paprika
2 tablespoons chopped ginger
2 teaspoons ground cinnamon
1 teaspoon saffron
2 bay leaves
3 tablespoons honey
10 pitted prunes

To Assemble
Cooked grains or cauliflower rice
Toasted almond slivers
Sesame seeds

For the Pork Chops
Preheat a water bath to 140°F (60°C).

Mix together the spices in a bowl. Lightly salt and pepper the pork chops then sprinkle with the spices. Place in a sous vide bag then seal the bag and cook for 2 to 3 hours, until heated through or pasteurized.

For the Tajine
Heat some oil in a pan over medium heat. Add the onions and cook until just starting to get tender. Add the orange juice, water, paprika, ginger, cinnamon, saffron, and bay leaves then bring to a simmer. Let simmer for 10 to 15 minutes until thickened. Remove from the heat and stir in the honey and prunes. Salt and pepper to taste.

To Assemble
Take the pork chops out of the water bath and remove them from the bag. Dry them thoroughly using paper towels or a dish cloth. Quickly sear the pork chops for 1 to 2 minutes per side, until just browned, then remove from the heat.

Place the cooked grains or cauliflower rice in a bowl or on a deep plate. Top with a pork chops and then spoon some of the tajine over the top. Sprinkle with the toasted almond slivers and sesame seeds then serve.

Rack of Lamb with Pomegranate and Brussels Sprouts

Cooks: 131°F (55°C) for 2 to 4 hours • Serves: 4
Nutritional: Cal 523; Fat 21g; Protein 43g; Carb 48g; Fiber 11g; Sugar 28g; Chol 105mg

Rack of lamb is a rich, flavorful cut to make so I try to lighten it up with the sides. Here I pair it with a zesty pomegranate sauce that cuts the richness while complimenting the strong lamb flavor. I also serve it with some Brussels sprouts and cherry tomatoes to bulk out the meal while cutting the richness of the lamb.

For the Rack of Lamb
1 rack of lamb, 1 ½ to 2 pounds
   (700 to 900 grams)
¼ teaspoon ground coriander
⅛ teaspoon ground cumin
Zest from ½ orange
1 sprig fresh rosemary

For the Pomegranate Sauce
2 cups pomegranate juice
¼ cup fresh orange juice
2 teaspoons fresh thyme leaves
1 ancho pepper, seeds
   and stem removed
1 cinnamon stick
1 tablespoon honey

For the Brussels Sprouts
1 ½ to 2 pounds Brussels sprouts
   (700 to 900 grams)
1 shallot, thinly sliced
2 tablespoons minced garlic
2 teaspoons fresh thyme leaves
2 tablespoons water
2 teaspoons lemon zest
¼ lemon

To Assemble
20 cherry tomatoes
2 tablespoons pomegranate seeds
3 tablespoons fresh oregano leaves
Smoked salt

For the Rack of Lamb

Preheat a water bath to 131°F (55°C).

Lightly salt the rack of lamb. Combine the coriander and cumin in a bowl then sprinkle over the lamb. Evenly spread the orange zest over the meat then place the lamb in a sous vide bag with the rosemary. Seal the bag and cook for 2 to 4 hours.

For the Pomegranate Sauce

Put the pomegranate juice, orange juice, thyme, ancho pepper and cinnamon in a pot over medium heat and lightly simmer for 20 to 30 minutes, until reduced and thickened. Remove from the heat, discard the cinnamon stick and ancho pepper then stir in the honey. The sauce can be made a day or two ahead of time and refrigerated, or left on the counter for an hour or two.

For the Brussels Sprouts

Cut the ends off of the Brussels sprouts and discard them. Cut the Brussels sprouts in half length-wise. Heat the olive oil in a pan over medium to medium-high heat. Add the Brussels sprouts and cook, stirring infrequently, until the Brussels sprouts start to brown.

Add the shallots, garlic, thyme, and water to the pan then cover it and let the Brussels sprouts steam until tender, 5 to 10 minutes. Remove the Brussels sprouts from the pan, toss with the lemon zest and squeeze the lemon over the top.

To Assemble

Remove the cooked rack of lamb from the bag, discarding the rosemary, and dry it off thoroughly using paper towels or a dish cloth. Quickly sear the lamb for 1 to 2 minutes per side, until just browned, then remove from the heat and cut it into serving sections, usually one or two ribs. Quickly sear the cherry tomatoes until they just burst.

Place a few sections of lamb onto the plate. Arrange the Brussels sprouts and roasted tomatoes around it. Drizzle the lamb with the pomegranate sauce. Add some pomegranate seeds and oregano leaves to the lamb, then sprinkle with some smoked salt.

Chicken Tikka Masala

Cooks: 141°F (60.5°C) for 2 to 4 hours • Serves: 4
Nutritional: Cal 314; Fat 13g; Protein 32g; Carb 20g; Fiber 6g; Sugar 13g; Chol 87mg

Chicken tikka masala is a traditional English dish at curry houses filled with rich flavors that connect on many different levels. My biggest problem with tikka masala is that the chicken is often dry and overcooked, which can be easily fixed by using sous vide. This results in meat that is always moist and tender.

There are many ingredients in this meal, but it comes together pretty quickly and there is always extra sauce that I freeze for later. If you prefer a richer tikka masala, you can stir in 1 cup of heavy cream after you simmer the tomatoes. I usually serve this with white rice or cauliflower rice.

For the Chicken
1 pound chicken breasts (450 grams)
¼ teaspoon garlic powder
¼ teaspoon ground coriander
⅛ teaspoon ginger powder
⅛ teaspoon ground turmeric
⅛ teaspoon cayenne pepper powder, or your chile powder of choice

For the Tikka Masala Sauce
1 onion, diced
4 cloves garlic, diced
1 tablespoon grated fresh ginger
1 jalapeño pepper, deseeded and diced
2 tablespoons tomato paste
2 tablespoons garam masala powder
2 tablespoons ground coriander
1 28-ounce can crushed tomatoes
1 tablespoon honey

To Assemble
4 dollops yogurt
¼ cup chopped fresh cilantro

For the Chicken
Preheat the water bath to 141°F (60.5°C).

Mix the spices together in a bowl. Salt and pepper the chicken then sprinkle with the spice mixture and seal in a sous vide bag. Place the sous vide bag in the water bath and cook for 2 to 4 hours, until pasteurized.

For the Tikka Masala Sauce
Heat oil in a pan over medium to medium-high heat. Add the onion and cook until softened, about 5 to 10 minutes. Add the garlic, ginger, and jalapeño pepper and cook for another 5 minutes.

Add the tomato paste, garam masala, and coriander then cook, stirring regularly, for 5 minutes. Add the crushed tomatoes then bring to a simmer for around 15 minutes. Blend well then stir in the honey, salt and pepper to taste then remove from the heat.

To Assemble
Take the chicken out of the sous vide bag. Dry them thoroughly using paper towels or a dish cloth. Quickly sear the chicken for 1 to 2 minutes per side, until just browned, then remove from the heat.

Place some sauce in a bowl, add the chicken to the sauce and top with a dollop of yogurt. Sprinkle with the cilantro then serve.

Chicken Mole in the Puebla Style

Cooks: 141°F (60.5°C) for 2 to 4 hours • Serves: 4
Nutritional: Cal 473; Fat 24g; Protein 34g; Carb 31g; Fiber 7g; Sugar 15g; Chol 87mg

When it is done right, Puebla-style mole is one of my favorite sauces. This recipe is for a more traditional preparation than the milder and cloyingly sweet versions found at chain restaurants. It takes advantage of the different chile flavors and is very bold and full flavored. The sauce does take a decent amount of effort, but I'll often double or triple the recipe and store the remainder in plastic bags in the freezer so I can easily use it later. The sauce also works exquisitely with shredded pork or chicken thighs.

I usually serve this with rice, beans, or corn, though I'll also sometimes go non-traditional and serve it with cauliflower rice or a farro and spelt grain mixture with some cilantro mixed in. For a completely different look, you can use this mole on a Mexican pizza instead of tomato sauce.

For the Chicken

1 pound chicken breasts (450 grams)
½ teaspoon garlic powder
¼ teaspoon onion powder
¼ teaspoon dried oregano

For the Mole

10 assorted medium-heat dried chile peppers such as ancho, mulato, chipotle, guajillo, and pasilla
2 cups chicken stock
½ onion, coarsely chopped
4 cloves garlic, coarsely chopped
1 medium tomato, quartered
1 medium tomatillo, quartered
3 tablespoons slivered almonds
2 tablespoons pumpkin seeds
2 tablespoons sesame seeds
1 teaspoon coriander seeds
½ teaspoon black peppercorns
½ teaspoon aniseed or fennel seed
2 whole cloves
2 tablespoons raisins
1 tablespoon ground cinnamon
2 tablespoons olive oil
1 to 2 ounces dark or unsweetened chocolate (28 to 56 grams)
1 tablespoon honey
1 tablespoon apple cider vinegar

To Assemble

2 avocados, sliced, optional
Sesame seeds
¼ cup fresh cilantro, chopped

For the Chicken

Preheat the water bath to 141°F (60.5°C).

Mix the spices together in a bowl. Salt and pepper the chicken then sprinkle with the spice mixture and seal in a sous vide bag. Place the sous vide bag in the water bath and cook for 2 to 4 hours, until pasteurized.

For the Mole

Preheat the broiler on an oven.

Remove the stems and seeds from the chile peppers. Discard the stems and half the seeds, reserving the others for later.

Heat some olive oil in a pan over medium high heat and sauté the deseeded chile peppers for 2 to 3 minutes per side. Remove and place in a blender or food processor with half the chicken stock.

Place some aluminum foil on a sheet pan with raised sides. Add the onion, garlic, tomato, and tomatillo then roast in the oven until they begin to blacken and soften, 15 to 30 minutes. Add them and their juices to the blender containing the chile peppers.

Toast the almonds, pumpkin seeds, sesame seeds, coriander, peppercorns, aniseed, cloves, and the reserved chile pepper seeds in a pan over medium heat until fragrant and just starting to brown, about 2 minutes. Add to the blender along with the raisins and cinnamon.

Once the mixture in the blender has cooled slightly, process it until it becomes a smooth paste, adding water if it is too thick.

Heat the olive oil in a large saucepan with high sides over medium heat. Add the puree from the food processor and cook for 5 minutes, stirring constantly, until it thickens. Reduce the heat to medium low and add the remaining chicken stock as well as the chocolate, honey and vinegar and stir to combine. Simmer the sauce for at least 10 minutes, and up to 50 minutes, while stirring occasionally until it becomes thick but still pourable. Salt and pepper to taste and then remove from the heat.

To Assemble

Take the chicken out of the water bath and remove it from the bag. Dry it off thoroughly using paper towels or a dish cloth. Quickly sear the chicken for 1 to 2 minutes per side, until just browned, then remove from the heat and place onto a plate.

Spoon the mole sauce over the chicken then top with the avocado slices. Sprinkle with the sesame seeds and cilantro then serve.

Turkey Curry with Cauliflower Pilaf

Cooks: 141°F (60.5°C) for 2 to 4 hours • Serves: 4
Nutritional: Cal 515; Fat 24g; Protein 38g; Carb 40g; Fiber 9g; Sugar 16g; Chol 64mg

I love a rich, flavorful curry served over rice, but to lighten it up I'll often use a cauliflower pilaf instead of white rice. The pilaf helps soak up the curry while cooking the turkey first with sous vide ensures that it comes out perfect every time. I like to use a Panang curry paste, but a typical green curry paste will work as well. The version isn't very veggie-heavy but I'll often add green beans, snow peas, asparagus, or broccoli to it.

For the Turkey

- 1 to 2 pounds turkey breast (450 to 900 grams)
- ½ teaspoon garlic powder
- ¼ teaspoon ground turmeric
- ¼ teaspoon mustard powder
- ⅛ teaspoon cayenne pepper powder

For the Curry

- 1 large onion, chopped
- 2 cloves garlic, minced
- 2 tablespoons Panang curry paste or other curry paste
- 1 cup coconut milk
- 1 cup chopped pineapple
- 1 ½ tablespoons fresh lime juice
- 1 tablespoon fish sauce
- 2 tablespoons brown sugar, optional

For the Cauliflower Pilaf

- 1 large head cauliflower, coarsely chopped
- ½ cup cooked peas
- ½ cup cooked corn kernels

To Assemble

- ½ cup roasted cashews, chopped
- 3 tablespoons chopped fresh basil leaves
- 1 serrano pepper, thinly sliced

For the Turkey

Preheat the water bath to 141°F (60.5°C).

Mix the spices together in a bowl. Salt and pepper the turkey then sprinkle with the spice mixture and seal in a sous vide bag. Place the sous vide bag in the water bath and cook for 2 to 4 hours, until pasteurized.

For the Curry

About 20 minutes before the turkey is done begin working on the curry.

Heat oil in a pan over medium heat. Add the onions, garlic, and curry paste then stir for 3 to 5 minutes, being careful not to burn it. Add the coconut milk and pineapple then bring to a simmer. Reduce the heat and cook for 15 minutes, until it is reduced and thick.

Remove the turkey from the sous vide bag and set aside. Add some of the juices from the bag to the pan with the coconut mixture and simmer for 5 more minutes. Add the lime juice, fish sauce and brown sugar then stir well to combine. Remove from the heat.

For the Cauliflower Pilaf

Place the florets in a food processor and pulse several times until they are the size of rice.

Heat some olive oil in a pan over high heat until it is just about to smoke. Add the cauliflower and fry until it just starts to brown, about 3 to 5 minutes. Mix in the peas and corn then remove from the heat.

To Assemble

Take the turkey out of the water bath and remove it from the bag. Dry it off thoroughly using paper towels or a dish cloth. Quickly sear the turkey for 1 to 2 minutes per side, until just browned, then remove from the heat and cut into slices or chunks.

Place some of the cauliflower pilaf in a bowl and spoon the curry over the top. Add the turkey to the top, sprinkle with the roasted cashews, basil leaves, and serrano slices then serve.

Main Dish Fish

Fish are still something I'm trying to get my head around! My wife loves fish, and while I like them, I'd rather spend the money on a great steak...but I'm a good husband so we eat fish pretty often!

I try to get creative when cooking fish, and I love to combine it with flavorful sides and sauces. It is a balancing act between adding flavor and overpowering the fish, but I think I've gotten pretty adept at walking that line.

Even if you aren't a fish person, I recommend you skim through the recipes and check out the sides and sauces, they all work nicely with meat as well...I should know, whenever there are leftovers I always put them on meat the next day!

Sealing Tip

Using a vacuum sealer to seal fish can badly smash it. Therefore, it's usually best to use a Ziploc Freezer Bag or, if your sealer has the ability, to only pull a light vacuum before sealing it.

Note: In these recipes I recommend the time and temperatures I prefer, but for more options you can refer to the "Common Temperature Ranges" section at the start of the "Recipes" chapter or the "Cooking by Tenderness" chapter.

Sea Bass with Mango Salsa

Cooks: 130°F (54.4°C) for 15 to 45 minutes • Serves: 4
Nutritional: Cal 352; Fat 14g; Protein 27g; Carb 33g; Fiber 4g; Sugar 24g; Chol 53mg

Flaky sea bass combines with a sweet and spicy mango salsa to create a light and refreshing summer dish that always reminds me of vacation. This recipe works well with most types of fish and the salsa is very versatile, even complimenting steak or chicken.

For the Sea Bass

4 sea bass portions, about 6 ounces each (170 grams)
2 tablespoons olive oil

For the Mango Salsa

2 mangoes, peeled and diced
1 shallot, sliced
½ serrano pepper, deseeded and diced
1 tablespoon fresh lime juice
1 tablespoon olive oil

For the Sautéed Kale

½ onion, thinly sliced
5 cloves of garlic, coarsely chopped
3 cups coarsely chopped, lightly packed kale
1 tablespoon white wine vinegar

To Assemble

¼ cup coarsely chopped fresh basil leaves

For the Sea Bass

Preheat a water bath to 130°F (54.4°C).

Salt and pepper the sea bass then place in the sous vide bag with the olive oil and lightly seal. Let the fish sit for 30 minutes for the dry brine to take effect then place in the water bath and cook for 15 to 45 minutes, until heated through.

For the Mango Salsa

Combine all the ingredients in a bowl.

For the Sautéed Kale

Heat some oil in a pan over medium to medium-high heat. Add the onion and cook until softened. Add the garlic and cook for 2 minutes. Add the kale and sauté until it wilts. Add the white wine vinegar and cover the pan. Cook until the kale is softened, adding water if needed to keep the inside of the pan moist.

To Assemble

Take the sea bass out of the bag and dry it thoroughly using paper towels or a dish cloth. Sear one side over high heat just until browned, 1 to 2 minutes. Remove from the heat.

Place some kale on a plate and top with the sea bass. Add a spoonful of the mango salsa and sprinkle with the chopped basil leaves then serve.

Mahi Mahi with Charmoula

Cooks: 130°F (54.4°C) for 15 to 45 minutes • Serves: 4
Nutritional: Cal 462; Fat 30g; Protein 34g; Carb 18g; Fiber 6g; Sugar 9g; Chol 124mg

Charmoula is a flavorful condiment used in several African countries such as Morocco and Libya. There are many variations of Charmoula and this recipe focuses on an herb-heavy version that I pair with mahi mahi. I serve it with a simple but flavorful vegetable medley that adds texture, color and base flavors to the dish. This version can be on the spicy side, so you can cut the serrano pepper in half if you prefer.

For the Mahi Mahi
4 mahi mahi portions, about 6 ounces each (170 grams)
½ teaspoon paprika
2 tablespoons olive oil

For the Charmoula
1 clove garlic, minced
½ cup chopped fresh parsley
¼ cup chopped fresh cilantro
¼ cup olive oil
Zest from 1 lemon
Juice from ½ lemon, about 1 tablespoon
1 serrano pepper, finely chopped
½ teaspoon ground cumin
½ teaspoon ground coriander

For the Vegetable Medley
2 carrots, diced
1 onion, diced
5 cloves garlic, minced
1 eggplant, diced
1 zucchini, diced
1 red bell pepper, diced
1 tablespoon fresh lemon juice

To Assemble
Zest from 1 lemon
¼ cup chopped fresh parsley

For the Mahi Mahi
Preheat a water bath to 130°F (54.4°C).

Salt and pepper the mahi mahi then sprinkle with the paprika. Place in the sous vide bag with the olive oil and lightly seal. Let the fish sit for 30 minutes for the dry brine to take effect then place in the water bath and cook for 15 to 45 minutes, until heated through.

For the Charmoula
Place all of the ingredients in a bowl and mix together.

For the Vegetable Medley
Heat some oil in a pan over medium to medium-high heat. Add the carrots and cook until they just begin to soften. Add the onion and cook until just softened. Add the garlic, eggplant, zucchini, and red pepper and cook until tender. Stir in the lemon juice then salt and pepper to taste.

To Assemble
Take the mahi mahi out of the bag and dry it thoroughly using paper towels or a dish cloth. Sear one side over high heat just until browned, 1 to 2 minutes. Remove from the heat.

Place some of the vegetable medley on a plate and top with the mahi mahi. Spoon the charmoula over the top. Sprinkle with the lemon zest and parsley then serve.

Swordfish with Bean and Corn Salad

Cooks: 130°F (54.4°C) for 15 to 45 minutes • Serves: 4
Nutritional: Cal 611; Fat 27g; Protein 45g; Carb 51g; Fiber 11g; Sugar 3g; Chol 112mg

Sous vide swordfish is one of the dishes my wife absolutely loves. Here I pair it with a simple but flavorful salad of beans, corn, collard greens and avocado rounded out with some lemon juice to brighten it up. I like to serve it with cooked farro, but you can use any grain you prefer, or even omit it if you want.

For the Swordfish
4 swordfish portions, about 6 ounces each (170 grams)
½ teaspoon garlic powder
¼ teaspoon ground cumin
¼ teaspoon ground coriander
2 tablespoons olive oil

For the Corn and Bean Salad
2 shallots, sliced
5 cloves garlic, minced
3 cups chopped collard greens
1 cup cooked corn kernels
1 cup cooked pinto beans
1 tablespoon fresh lemon juice
2 tablespoons chopped fresh basil leaves
1 avocado, diced, optional

To Assemble
2 cups cooked farro
1 lemon, cut into eighths

For the Swordfish
Preheat a water bath to 130°F (54.4°C).

Mix the spices together in a bowl. Salt and pepper the swordfish then sprinkle with the spice mixture. Place in the sous vide bag with the olive oil and lightly seal. Let the fish sit for 30 minutes for the dry brine to take effect then place in the water bath and cook for 15 to 45 minutes, until heated through.

For the Corn and Bean Salad
Heat some oil in a pan over medium to medium-high heat. Add the shallots and garlic and cook until just tender. Add the collard greens and cook until tender. Stir in the corn and pinto beans and warm through. Add the lemon juice, basil and avocado then remove from the heat.

To Assemble
Take the swordfish out of the bag and dry it thoroughly using paper towels or a dish cloth. Sear one side over high heat just until browned, 1 to 2 minutes. Remove from the heat.

Place some farro on a plate then top with the swordfish. Spoon some of the corn and bean salad over the top. Drizzle with the olive oil and serve with a lemon piece for squeezing over the top.

Swordfish with Romesco Sauce

Cooks: 130°F (54.4°C) for 15 to 45 minutes • Serves: 4
Nutritional: Cal 572; Fat 39g; Protein 43g; Carb 19g; Fiber 9g; Sugar 8g; Chol 112mg

Romesco sauce is a brightly flavored, quick to make sauce that is a go-to choice for me to use on all manner of meats and vegetables. It is made up of roasted red peppers, plum tomatoes, and almonds all blended together with a few spices. Here I like to serve it over swordfish and asparagus. Romesco sauce is very simple so try to use the most flavorful tomatoes you can find, it'll make a big difference!

For the Swordfish
4 swordfish portions, about 6 ounces each (170 grams)
½ teaspoon paprika
¼ teaspoon ground coriander
2 tablespoons olive oil

For the Romesco Sauce
½ cup roasted red peppers, coarsely chopped
3 tomatoes, preferably plum, coarsely chopped
½ cup roasted almonds
¼ cup fresh parsley
1 tablespoon olive oil
½ tablespoon paprika
¼ teaspoon cayenne pepper powder
2 cloves garlic
1 tablespoon fresh lemon juice

For the Asparagus
2 pounds asparagus, ends trimmed off (900 grams)
1 tablespoon minced garlic

To Assemble
Lemon zest
Basil leaves

For the Swordfish
Preheat a water bath to 130°F (54.4°C).

Mix the spices together in a bowl. Salt and pepper the swordfish then sprinkle with the spice mixture. Place in the sous vide bag with the olive oil and lightly seal. Let the fish sit for 30 minutes for the dry brine to take effect then place in the water bath and cook for 15 to 45 minutes, until heated through.

For the Romesco Sauce
Place two thirds of the red peppers and the 3 tomatoes into a blender. Add the almonds, parsley, olive oil, paprika, cayenne, garlic and lemon juice. Blend until relatively smooth. Salt and pepper to taste. Add the remaining red pepper and tomato then blend until just broken up.

For the Asparagus
Preheat an oven to 400°F (200°C).

Toss the asparagus and garlic with olive oil then salt and pepper it. Place on a roasting sheet then cook, stirring once or twice, about 20 to 30 minutes or until tender. Remove from the heat.

To Assemble
Take the swordfish out of the bag and dry it thoroughly using paper towels or a dish cloth. Sear one side over high heat just until browned, 1 to 2 minutes. Remove from the heat.

Place some asparagus on a plate and top with the swordfish. Spoon Romesco sauce on top and sprinkle with the lemon zest. Top with the basil leaves, drizzle with olive oil then serve.

Lobster Tail with Tomato and Corn Salad

Cooks: 131°F (55°C) for 20 to 40 minutes • Serves: 4
Nutritional: Cal 455; Fat 31g; Protein 29g; Carb 19g; Fiber 6g; Sugar 6g; Chol 191mg

Lobster cooked sous vide is tender and succulent, and this recipe showcases it with a simple tomato and corn salad. I prefer my lobster cooked at 131°F (55°C), but 140°F (60°C) will give you a more traditional texture. For a much softer texture you can drop the temperature lower.

To remove the lobster from the shell, you can either cut the shell off with kitchen shears, or boil the lobster for 1 to 2 minutes and chill it in an ice bath.

For the Lobster Tails
4 lobster tails, shell removed
4 tablespoons olive oil or butter, optional
8 fresh basil leaves

For the Tomato and Corn Salad
2 cups diced fresh tomatoes
1 cup cooked corn kernels
1 avocado, diced
8 fresh basil leaves
1 tablespoon fresh lemon juice
2 tablespoons olive oil

To Assemble
1 lemon, cut into eighths
Sea salt

For the Lobster Tails
Preheat a water bath to 131°F (55°C).

Place all the ingredients in a sous vide bag then seal. Cook until heated through, 20 to 40 minutes.

For the Tomato and Corn Salad
Combine all the ingredients in a bowl and toss well to combine. Salt and pepper to taste.

To Assemble
Place a large spoonful of the tomato and corn salad onto a plate. Remove the lobster from the sous vide bag and place one on top of the tomato salad. Spoon some of the butter out of the sous vide bag onto the lobster. Squeeze some lemon over the top, sprinkle with the sea salt and then serve.

Squid Puttanesca with Summer Squash Noodles

Cooks: 138°F (58.9°C) for 2 to 4 hours • Serves: 4
Nutritional: Cal 302; Fat 16g; Protein 24g; Carb 17g; Fiber 5g; Sugar 7g; Chol 215mg

Puttanesca is a hearty, full-flavored sauce that packs a huge punch. I pair it with some sous vided squid that adds some extra texture to the dish. This sauce can also stand up to many proteins and I'll often use it on beef or lamb. This is a really salty dish so if you are trying to lower your salt intake it might not be right for you.

I love a traditional version served over spaghetti but sometimes I like to lighten it up and use summer squash like zucchini as the "pasta" base. You can either cut the zucchini into matchsticks or thin slivers, or use a mandolin or spiralizer to make longer noodle shapes.

I usually use Kalamata or other high-quality brined olives. If you can find them with the pits removed it will also greatly speed up your prep work. You can also sear the squid if you like, which will firm it up slightly.

For the Squid
¾ pound squid, cleaned and cut into rings (340 grams)
1 teaspoon garlic powder
1 teaspoon fresh thyme leaves
¼ teaspoon red pepper flakes

For the Puttanesca Sauce
3 tablespoons olive oil
5 cloves garlic, minced
4 anchovy fillets, finely minced
½ teaspoon red pepper flakes
3 tablespoons chopped capers
¼ cup chopped olives
1 ½ cup crushed tomatoes
¼ cup chopped fresh parsley

To Assemble
2 zucchini or other summer squash, cut into matchsticks or spiralized
Zest from 1 lemon
¼ cup chopped fresh parsley
Red pepper flakes

For the Squid
Preheat a water bath to 138°F (58.9°C).

Mix the spices together in a bowl. Salt and pepper the squid then sprinkle with some of the spice mixture. Add to the sous vide bag, lightly seal, and place in the water bath. Cook the squid for 2 to 4 hours.

For the Puttanesca Sauce
Add the oil, garlic, anchovies and red pepper flakes to a pan and heat over medium heat. Once the garlic just starts to brown add the capers, olives, and crushed tomatoes. Bring the mixture to a simmer and let it simmer until it thickens to your desired consistency. Remove from the heat and stir in the parsley.

To Assemble
Remove the squid from the sous vide bag. Place a mound of the zucchini on a plate and top with a spoonful or two of the puttanesca sauce. Add some squid to the top then sprinkle with the lemon zest, parsley, and some red pepper flakes. Drizzle some olive oil on the top then serve.

Citrus Cured Salmon with Fennel Carpaccio

Cooks: 110°F (43°C) for 15 to 45 minutes • Serves: 4
Nutritional: Cal 306; Fat 13g; Protein 28g; Carb 22g; Fiber 3g; Sugar 17g; Chol 59mg

Lightly curing salmon infuses it with flavor and contributes a firmness of texture. Once it has been cured, I like to cook it at 110°F (43°C) to give it some structure without drying it out any. It's then chilled and sliced thinly before being served on top of a fennel carpaccio. It's a bright, citrusy dish that is great as a light main course on a spring day or as an appetizer to share.

For the Salmon
1 pound salmon (450 grams)
Zest from 1 lemon
Zest from 1 lime
Zest from 1 orange
2 tablespoons salt
2 tablespoons white sugar

For the Fennel Carpaccio
1 fennel bulb
2 tablespoons fresh orange juice
1 tablespoon fresh lemon juice
2 tablespoons olive oil

For the Pickled Onions
1 red onion, thinly sliced
¼ cup red wine vinegar
¼ cup water
1 tablespoon sugar, optional

To Assemble
2 tablespoons capers
Zest from 1 lemon
Zest from 1 lime
Zest from 1 orange
Reserved fennel fronds, chopped
Sea salt

For the Salmon
Preheat a water bath to 110°F (43°C).

Remove the pin bones and skin from the salmon. Sprinkle the salmon with the citrus zest. Combine the salt and sugar together in a small bowl then sprinkle some over the salmon, there will be some left over. Place the salmon in the sous vide bag and lightly seal. Let the fish sit in the refrigerator for at least 30 minutes but preferably several hours for the dry brine to take effect. Place the sous vide bag in the water bath and cook for 15 to 45 minutes, until heated through.

Once cooked, remove the sous vide bag from the water bath and place in an ice bath until chilled.

For the Fennel Carpaccio
Remove the root of the fennel. Remove the fronds and reserve them, then thinly slice the fennel.

Add the orange juice, lemon juice, and olive oil to a bowl then whisk to combine. Add the fennel and toss to coat.

For the Pickled Onions
Add the onion, red wine vinegar, water, and sugar to a pot and bring to a boil. Reduce the heat and let simmer for 5 minutes. Remove from the heat and let cool.

To Assemble
Take the cooked and chilled salmon out of sous vide bag and pat dry. Thinly slice the salmon.

Place some of the fennel carpaccio on a plate along with its dressing. Top with several slices of salmon. Add some capers then sprinkle with the citrus zest. Top with some fennel fronds and pickled red onion. Sprinkle with sea salt then serve.

Halibut with Chimichurri and Tomato Salad

Cooks: 130°F (54.4°C) for 15 to 45 minutes • Serves: 4
Nutritional: Cal 603; Fat 49g; Protein 34g; Carb 12g; Fiber 4g; Sugar 4g; Chol 83mg

Halibut is a light but flavorful fish; combining it with an herby chimichurri and an acidic tomato salad helps highlight the flavors. Chimichurri is a garlic and parsley based sauce and is very popular in many South American countries. Most chimichurri is pretty oily but I halved the olive oil in this recipe, if you prefer a more traditional style you can increase it to a full cup.

For the Halibut

4 halibut portions, about 6 ounces each (170 grams)

½ teaspoon garlic powder

½ teaspoon paprika

2 tablespoons olive oil

For the Chimichurri Sauce

2 cups chopped fresh parsley

2 tablespoons fresh oregano leaves

6 cloves garlic, coarsely chopped

1 tablespoons red wine vinegar

2 tablespoons fresh lime juice

½ cup olive oil

1 teaspoon paprika

½ jalapeño, deseeded and coarsely diced

For the Tomato and Onion Salad

2 cloves garlic, minced

2 tablespoons sherry vinegar

3 tablespoons olive oil

1 pint cherry tomatoes, halved

¼ sweet onion, thinly sliced

½ red bell pepper, cut into thin strips

2 tablespoons chopped fresh basil leaves

To Assemble

¼ cup chopped fresh parsley

For the Halibut

Preheat a water bath to 130°F (54.4°C).

Mix the spices together in a bowl. Salt and pepper the halibut then sprinkle with the spice mixture. Place in the sous vide bag with the olive oil and lightly seal. Let the fish sit for 30 minutes for the dry brine to take effect then place in the water bath and cook for 15 to 45 minutes, until heated through.

For the Chimichurri Sauce

Combine all the ingredients in a blender or food processor and process until combined well.

For the Tomato and Onion Salad

Combine the garlic and vinegar in a bowl and let sit for 5 minutes. Add the olive oil and whisk to combine. Toss the remaining ingredients with the dressing.

To Assemble

Take the halibut out of the bag and dry it thoroughly using paper towels or a dish cloth. Sear one side over high heat just until browned, 1 to 2 minutes. Remove from the heat.

Place some of the tomato and onion salad on a plate and top with the halibut. Drizzle some chimichurri sauce on the top then sprinkle with parsley and serve.

Scallops with Tabbouleh Salad

Cooks: 122°F (50°C) for 15 to 35 minutes • Serves: 4
Nutritional: Cal 231; Fat 12g; Protein 17g; Carb 17g; Fiber 4g; Sugar 3g; Chol 27mg

Tabbouleh is a very herbaceous salad from the Middle East that is largely parsley and mint based. It has some bulgur in it to bulk it out and some lemon juice and tomatoes to add acidity with a little sweet onion to complete the suite of flavors. Many recipes call for cold soaking the bulgur with the tomato juices and some extra water but here I just call for pre-cooked bulgur to make it simpler.

Tabbouleh is often eaten by itself, on lettuce leaves, or with warm pitas, but here I like to serve it alongside scallops to add flavor to them without overpowering the delicate scallop flavor.

For the Scallops
1 pound large scallops (450 grams)
¼ teaspoon allspice
¼ teaspoon ground coriander

For the Tabbouleh Salad
3 cups well dried and finely chopped fresh flat leaf parsley
1 cup well dried and finely chopped fresh mint
½ cup cooked / hydrated bulgur, well drained
2 medium tomatoes, diced
2 tablespoons fresh lemon juice
⅛ sweet onion, minced
3 tablespoons olive oil

To Assemble
Fresh mint leaves

For the Scallops
Preheat the water bath to 122°F (50°C).

Mix the spices together in a bowl. Salt and pepper the scallops then sprinkle with the spice mixture. Add to the sous vide bag in a single layer then lightly seal. Place the sous vide bag in the water bath and cook for 15 to 35 minutes.

For the Tabbouleh Salad
Mix together all the ingredients in a large bowl.

To Assemble
Remove the scallops from the sous vide bag and dry them thoroughly using paper towels or a dish cloth. Sear over high heat on one side until they just begin to brown. Remove from the heat.

Spoon some tabbouleh salad on a plate then top with the scallops. Top with some mint leaves then serve.

Soy Sauce Cured Pollock with Green Apple Salad

Cooks: 130°F (54.4°C) for 15 to 45 minutes • Serves: 4
Nutritional: Cal 301; Fat 7g; Protein 38g; Carb 21g; Fiber 6g; Sugar 11g; Chol 121mg

Pollock is an inexpensive, mild fish very similar to cod or haddock, both of which can be used in this recipe. To bump up the flavors, I like to replace the usual dry brine I use on fish with a wet brine utilizing soy sauce, fish sauce, and miso paste. It adds a bunch of flavor while firming up the fish for cooking. If you can't seal liquids, you can let the fish sit in the brine to cure and then pour out the brine before sealing.

The wet brine makes the fish a little on the salty side so I like to pair it with a tart and spicy green apple salad. It's my take on a green papaya salad and incorporates many of the flavors of that traditional Thai dish into a simple everyday side.

For the Pollock
4 pollock portions, about 6 ounces each (170 grams)
2 tablespoons soy sauce
2 teaspoons fish sauce
2 teaspoons miso paste

For the Green Apple Salad
2 Granny Smith apples
12 green beans
2 cloves garlic, minced
1 serrano pepper, deseeded and minced
1 tablespoon fish sauce
1 tablespoon fresh lime juice
½ cup shredded carrots
8 cherry tomatoes, halved

To Assemble
¼ cup chopped fresh cilantro
¼ cup coarsely chopped roasted peanuts

For the Halibut
Preheat a water bath to 130°F (54.4°C).

Mix the soy sauce, fish sauce, and miso paste together to form a wet brine. Pepper the pollock then brush liberally with the wet brine. Place in the sous vide bag then lightly seal. Let the fish sit for 30 to 60 minutes for the brine to take effect then place in the water bath and cook for 15 to 45 minutes, until heated through.

For the Green Apple Salad
Clean the outside of the apples and remove the cores. Cut them into matchsticks, or use a mandolin or spiralizer. Clean the green beans, cut them into 2" long pieces (50mm) then cut into quarters lengthwise.

Mix together the garlic, serrano pepper, fish sauce and lime juice. Toss mixture with the green apple, green beans, and shredded carrots. Salt and pepper to taste then stir in the cherry tomatoes.

To Assemble
Take the pollock out of the bag and pat dry.

Place some of the green apple salad on a plate and top with the pollock. Add the cilantro and roasted peanuts then serve.

Sides and Vegetables

Sous vide is usually known for its transformative effect on meat, but it also does an amazing job with vegetables!

Vegetables almost always need to be cooked above 183°F (83.9°C) for them to break down, and that's what most of my recipes use. The timing for vegetables is more critical than with meat but you do have greater leeway than when using traditional methods.

Most of the vegetables in this chapter can be used as sides or even as the star of a meal.

Note: In these recipes I recommend the time and temperatures I prefer, but for more options you can refer to the "Common Temperature Ranges" section at the start of the "Recipes" chapter or the "Cooking by Tenderness" chapter.

Beets and Goat Cheese

Cooks: 183°F (83.9°C) for 60 to 90 Minutes • Serves: 4 as a side
Nutritional: Cal 350; Fat 23g; Protein 17g; Carb 22g; Fiber 7g; Sugar 13g; Chol 28mg

Earthy beets are a great combination with bright oranges and rich goat cheese. It is rounded out with some sweet balsamic vinegar and woody toasted walnut. Beets stain so be sure to cover your cutting board with parchment paper or plastic wrap. I also wear plastic gloves to save my hands from turning red.

For the Beets
8 beets
Zest from 1 orange

To Assemble
2 tablespoons chopped fresh tarragon
Zest from 1 orange
1 shallot, thinly sliced
2 cups lightly packed arugula
1 cup crumbled goat cheese, preferably Chevre
½ cup walnuts
Balsamic vinegar

For the Beets
Preheat the water bath to 183°F (83.9°C).

Peel the beets and cut them into bite-sized chunks. Zest the orange over the beets then salt and pepper them. Place the beets in a sous vide bag, trying to keep the thickness of the bag less than 1" (25mm) for even cooking. Seal the bag and cook for 60 to 90 minutes, until heated through and tender.

To Assemble
Remove the beets from the bag and toss with the tarragon, orange zest, shallot, and arugula. Top with some goat cheese and walnuts then drizzle with the balsamic vinegar and serve.

Sesame-Miso Bok Choy

Cooks: 183°F (83.9°C) for 15 to 30 minutes • Serves: 4 as a side
Nutritional: Cal 113; Fat 9g; Protein 3g; Carb 5g; Fiber 2g; Sugar 1g; Chol 0mg

Bok choy isn't too hard to cook traditionally, but with sous vide it can be tenderized without making it overly soft. It also completely eliminates the cleanup since you don't have to pull out a pot or pan. If you prefer a thicker sauce you can always reduce it on the stove after the sous vide process is complete.

For the Bok Choy
- 4 baby bok choy
- 1 tablespoon olive oil
- 1 tablespoon freshly grated ginger
- 1 tablespoon miso paste
- 1 tablespoon soy sauce
- Salt and pepper

To Assemble
- Fish sauce
- Sesame oil
- Sesame seeds

For the Bok Choy

Preheat the water bath to 183°F (83.9°C).

Combine all ingredients in a bowl and toss to mix well. Pour into a sous vide bag and arrange in a single layer. Seal the bag then place in the water bath and cook for 15 to 30 minutes.

Once the bok choy is tender remove it from the water bath.

To Assemble

Remove the bok choy from the sous vide bag and place in a bowl. Drizzle with some fish sauce and sesame oil. Sprinkle with the sesame seeds then serve.

Dill Pickles

Cooks: 140°F (60°C) for 2 to 3 hours • Makes: 2 pints pickles
Nutritional: Cal 32; Fat 2g; Protein 1g; Carb 5g; Fiber 1g; Sugar 2g; Chol 0mg

Crisp, tart pickles are a constant in my refrigerator but many store-bought brands are filled with sweeteners and stabilizers. Making pickles at home allows you to use only the ingredients you want and they are especially tasty when cucumbers are in season at the farmers market.

Due to the low temperature, the vegetables really don't soften, so this recipe works best with more tender vegetables like cucumbers, summer squash, berries, or peppers. If you don't like dill pickles, you can replace the dill with other herbs or spices like rosemary, red pepper flakes, or sage.

I first saw this time and temperature combination on ChefSteps and it works wonderfully. They claim the pickles will last unrefrigerated for up to 6 months but I've never tested that myself.

For the Brine
1 cup water
1 cup white wine vinegar
3 tablespoons sugar, optional
1 tablespoon salt

For the Pickles
1 ½ pints cucumber spears
¼ red onion, thinly sliced
7 sprigs fresh dill
2 teaspoons black peppercorns
2 teaspoons whole coriander seeds

For the Brine
Combine all the ingredients in a bowl and whisk until the sugar and salt dissolve.

For the Pickles
Preheat the water bath to 140°F (60°C).

Place the cucumber spears, onions and fresh dill into two 1-pint Mason jars, leaving some room at the top. Add the peppercorns and coriander seeds. Fill the jar with enough brine to cover the vegetables while still leaving some space at the top. Place the lid on the jar and finger tighten it. Place the jar in the water bath and cook for 2 to 3 hours.

Once the pickles are cooked, remove the Mason jar from the water bath and let cool on the counter or in a room-temperature water bath. Place in the refrigerator and use as desired.

Spicy Rosemary Pickled Carrots

Cooks: 183°F (83.9°C) for 30 to 45 minutes • Makes: 1 pint pickles
Nutritional: Cal 35; Fat 0g; Protein 1g; Carb 7g; Fiber 2g; Sugar 3g; Chol 0mg

This pickling recipe uses a higher temperature to soften up the vegetables. It works great with carrots, green beans, and other tougher vegetables. The timing varies based on the vegetable, but following the general guidelines in the Cooking by Tenderness chapter will help give you an idea, though I usually go a little shorter so the vegetables have more crunch to them. You can also mix up the spices and herbs to create your own flavor profiles.

For the Brine
½ cup water
½ cup white wine vinegar
2 tablespoons sugar, optional
½ tablespoon salt

For the Pickles
1 pint carrot sticks
2 sprigs fresh rosemary
½ teaspoon black peppercorns
½ teaspoon whole cumin seeds
½ teaspoon red pepper flakes

For the Brine
Combine all the ingredients in a bowl and whisk until the sugar and salt dissolve.

For the Pickles
Preheat the water bath to 183°F (83.9°C).

Place the carrots sticks and rosemary in a pint Mason jar, leaving some room at the top. Add the peppercorns, cumin seeds and red pepper flakes. Fill the jar with enough brine to cover the vegetables while still leaving some space at the top. Place the lid on the jar and finger tighten it. Place the jar in the water bath and cook for 30 to 45 minutes.

Once the pickles are cooked, remove the Mason jar from the water bath and let cool on the counter, or in a room-temperature water bath. Place in the refrigerator and use as desired.

Asparagus with Garlic-Shallot Oil

Cooks: 183°F (83.9°C) for 10 to 30 Minutes • Serves: 4 as a side
Nutritional: Cal 201; Fat 18g; Protein 5g; Carb 10g; Fiber 5g; Sugar 5g; Chol 0mg

Asparagus can be cooked many different ways, but using sous vide can remove most of the timing pressure. I especially like using sous vide on the thicker asparagus, since the lower temperature allows it to cook through without overcooking the outsides. For this recipe I like to combine the cooked asparagus with some olive oil infused with shallots and garlic then top it all off with some tarragon and lemon zest.

For the Asparagus
2 bunches asparagus, ends trimmed off

For the Garlic-Shallot Oil
5 tablespoons olive oil
2 shallots, thinly sliced
4 cloves garlic, minced
⅛ teaspoon red pepper flakes

To Assemble
3 tablespoons chopped fresh tarragon leaves
Zest from 1 lemon

For the Asparagus
Preheat the water bath to 183°F (83.9°C).

Salt and pepper the asparagus and put in the sous vide bag. Seal the bag and place it in the water bath. Cook the asparagus for 10 to 30 minutes, until heated through and tender.

For the Garlic-Shallot Oil
Combine all the ingredients in a pot over medium heat. Heat until the shallots and garlic just begin to sizzle then reduce the heat and let steep for about 15 minutes.

To Assemble
Remove the asparagus from the bag and place on a plate. Spoon the shallot oil, along with the shallots and garlic, on top. Sprinkle with the tarragon and lemon zest then serve.

Miso Glazed Turnips

Cooks: 183°F (83.9°C) for 45 to 60 minutes • Serves: 4 as a side
Nutritional: Cal 101; Fat 4g; Protein 2g; Carb 17g; Fiber 2g; Sugar 13g; Chol 0mg

Using sous vide to glaze turnips is a simple process that results in a great side dish, especially when combined with umami-rich miso. You can also briefly cook turnips and their juices in a pan after sous viding them to reduce the sauce for a richer dish. This recipe also works well for other root vegetables such as carrots, radishes, and parsnips.

For the Turnips

2 to 4 turnips, peeled and cut into 1" wedges (25 mm)
1 tablespoon miso
1 tablespoon butter or olive oil
1 teaspoon sweet paprika

To Assemble

2 tablespoons honey
Juice from ¼ lemon
Zest from 1 lemon
2 scallions, sliced

For the Turnips

Preheat the water bath to 183°F (83.9°C).

Combine all ingredients in a bowl and toss to mix well. Pour into a sous vide bag, trying to keep the thickness of the bag less than 1" (25mm) for even cooking, and seal. Place in the water bath and cook for 45 to 60 minutes.

Once the turnips are tender remove them from the water bath.

To Assemble

Pour the turnips and their juices into a pan and heat over medium-high heat until the juices have thickened. Drizzle with the honey and sprinkle with the lemon juice. Cook until the sauce has thickened. Remove from the heat and serve with some lemon zest and scallions on top.

Sous Vide Poached Cherry Tomatoes

Cooks: 131°F (55°C) for 30 minutes • Serves: 4 to 8 as a side
Nutritional: Cal 149; Fat 14g; Protein 2g; Carb 6g; Fiber 2g; Sugar 4g; Chol 0mg

Using sous vide to lightly poach tomatoes results in a tender and moist side dish. The tomatoes are just heated through, not broken down, so cooking them at almost any low temperature works well. I usually serve them with steaks so I cook them at 131°F (55°C) because I toss them in with the steaks at the end of their cooking time.

For the Cherry Tomatoes
- 2 pints cherry tomatoes
- 4 tablespoons good olive oil
- 1 tablespoon chopped fresh rosemary leaves
- 1 tablespoon fresh thyme leaves
- Salt and pepper

For the Cherry Tomatoes

At least 30 minutes before serving

Preheat a water bath to 131°F (55°C).

Put the cherry tomatoes, olive oil, rosemary and thyme in a sous vide bag and mix together well, trying to keep the thickness of the bag less than 1" (25mm) for even cooking. Salt and pepper the tomatoes then seal the bag. Cook the tomatoes for 30 minutes.

Once cooked, remove the tomatoes from the sous vide bag, place in a bowl and serve as a side.

Spicy Street Corn

Cooks: 183°F (83.9°C) for 15 to 25 minutes • Serves: 4 as a side
Nutritional: Cal 144; Fat 6g; Protein 6g; Carb 2g; Fiber 3g; Sugar 8g; Chol 17mg

The sweetness of fresh corn combined with the kick of ancho pepper powder with some sourness from feta cheese and lime zest makes for an amazing between-meals snack. This whole dish hinges on the corn, so the sweeter you can find the better. Corn can vary widely in its tenderness, so it's often best to try a kernel raw before cooking it. This will give you an idea of how sweet and tender it already is and can inform your cooking time.

For the Corn
4 ears of corn

To Assemble
Ancho pepper powder
2 limes, for zesting
⅓ cup crumbled feta cheese
3 tablespoons finely chopped fresh cilantro

For the Corn
Preheat the water bath to 183°F (83.9°C).

Remove the husks from the corn and discard. Place the corn into the sous vide bag in a single layer. Seal the bag and cook them for around 15 to 25 minutes until tender.

To Assemble
Remove the corn from the sous vide bag. Salt and pepper the corn then lightly sprinkle with the ancho pepper powder. Zest the lime over the top, crumble the feta cheese on the corn and top with the fresh cilantro then serve.

Southwestern Sweet Potato Salad

Cooks: 183°F (83.9°C) for 45 to 60 minutes • Serves: 4 as a side
Nutritional: Cal 281; Fat 12g; Protein 6g; Carb 40g; Fiber 7g; Sugar 8g; Chol 0mg

The sweetness of sweet potatoes is perfectly offset by the spices and poblano pepper in this recipe, resulting in a complex mix of flavors that is a great addition to many meals. You can serve this alongside almost any protein, but chicken and turkey are my go-to proteins with it. I also will take this when we do potluck dinners with friends since it travels well.

For the Sweet Potatoes
2 sweet potatoes
½ teaspoon ground coriander
½ teaspoon paprika
½ teaspoon ground cloves
½ teaspoon ancho pepper powder

To Assemble
3 tablespoons olive oil
1 ½ cups corn kernels, cooked
1 ½ cups canned black-eyed peas, rinsed and drained
¼ red onion, diced
1 poblano pepper, diced
½ cup chopped fresh cilantro
Juice from 2 limes

For the Sweet Potatoes
Preheat a water bath to 183°F (83.9°C).

Peel the sweet potatoes and cut into ½" to 1" chunks (13mm to 25mm). Add them to the sous vide bag along with the spices and mix together well. Seal and cook for 45 to 60 minutes until the potatoes are soft.

To Assemble
Heat the oil, corn, black-eyed peas, onion, and pepper in a pan over medium heat. Once hot, remove the pan from the heat and stir in the cilantro and lime juice.

Remove the sweet potatoes from the sous vide bag and add to the pan with the vegetables. Toss well to combine then serve.

Cauliflower and Chickpeas

Cooks: 183°F (83.9°C) for 20 to 30 minutes • Serves: 4 as a side
Nutritional: Cal 222; Fat 9g; Protein 9g; Carb 30g; Fiber 9g; Sugar 8g; Chol 0mg

Cauliflower might be on the bland side, but combined with chickpeas, cherry tomatoes and red bell pepper, it turns into a flavorful and filling side. With the addition of tart lime juice and spicy jalapeño pepper it's a complex dish that comes together in no time.

For the Cauliflower
1 head of cauliflower, cut into florets
½ teaspoon cayenne pepper powder

To Assemble
2 tablespoons olive oil
¾ cup diced red bell pepper
1 jalapeño pepper, deseeded and diced
3 cloves garlic, minced
1 ½ cups cooked chickpeas
1 ½ cups halved cherry tomatoes
3 tablespoons fresh lime juice
½ cup lightly packed chopped fresh basil leaves

For the Cauliflower

Preheat a water bath to 183°F (83.9°C).

Sprinkle the cauliflower with the cayenne pepper powder then place in the sous vide bag. Salt and pepper the cauliflower and then seal the bag. Place the bag into the water bath and cook for 20 to 30 minutes, until soft.

To Assemble

Heat the oil, peppers, garlic, and chickpeas in a pan over medium heat. Once hot, remove the pan from the heat and stir in the cherry tomatoes, lime juice, and basil.

Remove the cauliflower from the sous vide bag and add to the pan with the vegetables. Toss well to combine then serve.

Infusions

Sous vide works wonders for making infusions. Higher temperatures are used when making sous vide infusions, which means that the flavors are extracted much faster than they are during traditional infusions, which are done at room temperature.

A sous vide infusion is also made in a sealed container such as a Mason jar, glass bottle, or plastic bag. This prevents evaporation and flavor loss, keeping the flavors of the infusion concentrated.

The temperature used can also be tightly controlled because of the high precision of sous vide machines, determining how much the liquid and flavoring agents are cooked from the heat.

Most infusions are made between 131°F to 160°F (55°C to 71.1°C) for vinegar, water or alcohol and 149°F to 176°F (65°C to 80°C) for oils. The temperature used affects the flavor profile of the infusion as different essences are extracted more quickly from the flavoring agents at various temperatures.

They are usually sous vided for 1 to 4 hours for vinegar or alcohol and 3 to 12 hours for oil, depending on the temperature used and the flavor profile desired.

Once the infusion has been completed it should be chilled in an ice bath so the volatile aromatics will return to the liquid. Once chilled, strain the liquid and then it is ready to be used. I've never had a jar crack on me, but if you run into trouble with that, you can place it in a room temperature bath for a few minutes to lower the temperature before using the ice bath.

Note: There is no nutritional information available for the infusions, as the main ingredients are all strained out.

Orange Fennel Vinegar

Cooks: 155°F (68.3°C) for 1 to 2 hours • Makes 1 ½ cups

Infused vinegars are a great way to add subtle flavors to vinaigrettes and sauces. Several infused vinegars are available in stores but they are often much more expensive than their plain counterparts. Making your own at home is quick and easy, plus much less expensive.

In this recipe the bright citrus notes pull out the sweetness and licorice flavor of the fennel, resulting in a floral, flavorful vinegar. This vinegar is great drizzled on fish or used to brighten up vegetables.

For the Orange Fennel Infusion
1 orange
½ fennel bulb, coarsely chopped
1 ½ cups white wine vinegar

For the Orange Fennel Infusion
Preheat a water bath to 155°F (68.3°C).

Lightly scrub the outside of the orange then remove the zest with a vegetable peeler or zester. Make sure little to no pith came off as well, using a paring knife to remove any.

Combine the orange zest, chopped fennel, and vinegar in a Mason jar or glass bottle then seal. Infuse in the water bath for 1 to 2 hours.

Prepare an ice bath with ½ ice and ½ water. Remove the bag or Mason jar from the water bath and place in the ice bath for 15 to 20 minutes. Strain the infusion and store in a sealed container. It will last for several weeks in the refrigerator.

Blackberry Peach Vinegar

Cooks: 140°F (60°C) for 1 to 2 hours • Makes 1 ½ cups

Every summer I have tons of blackberries and peaches that I'm looking to cook with. I can only make so many chutneys and sauces so I like to preserve their bright flavors by making infused vinegars with them. I use this vinegar to drizzle on salads or make tasty shrubs by mixing it with club soda and some honey. I call for white wine vinegar but I also enjoy the sweeter flavor of white balsamic vinegar sometimes.

For the Blackberry Peach Infusion
¾ cup coarsely chopped blackberries
¾ peach, coarsely chopped
1 ½ cups white wine vinegar
½ teaspoon whole cloves

For the Blackberry Peach Infusion

Preheat a water bath to 140°F (60°C).

Combine all of the ingredients in a sous vide bag or Mason jar then seal. Infuse in the water bath for 2 to 4 hours.

Prepare an ice bath with ½ ice and ½ water. Remove the bag or Mason jar from the water bath and place in the ice bath for 15 to 20 minutes. Strain the infusion and store in a sealed container. It will last for several weeks in the refrigerator.

Flavors of Tuscany Olive Oil

Cooks: 155°F (68.3°C) for 1 to 2 hours • Makes 1 ½ cups

Whenever we go to a nice Italian restaurant I start drooling just thinking about bread fresh from the oven with rich olive oil to dip it in. Some places also season the oil with fresh herbs, making it even more flavorful. This infusion encapsulates many of the traditional flavors of Tuscan cooking in a rich and bold olive oil. You're on your own for the fresh bread though!

When making oil infusions, be sure to thoroughly clean the flavoring agents before using them. The infusion process doesn't usually have any effect on bacteria that may be present so there is always a risk of botulism or other bacterial infections. After washing, dry the flavoring agents thoroughly to make sure no water is introduced or it can become rancid.

For the Tuscany Olive Oil
- 15 fresh basil leaves
- 3 tablespoons fresh marjoram
- 2 tablespoons fresh oregano leaves
- 2 tablespoons fresh thyme leaves
- 2 tablespoons fresh rosemary
- ½ teaspoon red pepper flakes
- 1 ½ cups olive oil

For the Tuscany Olive Oil

Preheat a water bath to 155°F (68.3°C).

Combine all the ingredients in a Mason jar or glass bottle then seal. Infuse in the water bath for 1 to 2 hours.

Prepare an ice bath with ½ ice and ½ water. Remove the bag or Mason jar from the water bath and place in the ice bath for 15 to 20 minutes. Strain the infusion and store in a sealed container. It will last for several weeks in the refrigerator.

Lemon Tarragon Olive Oil

Cooks: 155°F (68.3°C) for 1 to 2 hours • Makes 1 ½ cups

Infusing oils with different flavors is a wonderful way to add nuance and flavor to dishes. Oils can be lightly flavored, only adding background notes, or they can be full of flavors and be the highlight of a dish. I like to make this flavorful infused oil so I can drizzle it over fish or steak. The brightness of the lemon compliments the tarragon while the shallots contribute a little sweetness.

For the Lemon Tarragon Oil
Zest of 1 lemon
½ cup fresh tarragon leaves
1 shallot, minced
1 ½ cups olive oil

For the Lemon Tarragon Oil

Preheat a water bath to 155°F (68.3°C).

Lightly scrub the outside of the lemon then remove the zest with a vegetable peeler or zester. Make sure little to no pith came off as well, using a paring knife to remove any.

Combine the lemon zest with the remaining ingredients in a Mason jar or glass bottle then seal. Infuse in the water bath for 1 to 2 hours.

Prepare an ice bath with ½ ice and ½ water. Remove the bag or Mason jar from the water bath and place in the ice bath for 15 to 20 minutes. Strain the infusion and store in a sealed container. It will last for several weeks in the refrigerator.

Cherry Vanilla Soda Mixer Concentrate

Cooks: 160°F (71.1°C) for 2 to 4 hours • Makes: 3 cups mix

Cherry and vanilla are a classic flavor combination and they complement each other wonderfully in this soda mixer. I call for both sour and sweet dried cherries but if you only have access to one kind it will be fine. I use this in the same way as the upcoming Root Beer Soda Mixer infusion, though if I'm making a syrup I will add 1 cup of white sugar instead of the heavier brown sugar.

For the Cherry Vanilla Soda Mixer

Zest from 1 lemon
3 cups water
2 vanilla beans, split lengthwise
1 cinnamon stick
½ cup packed dried cherries
½ cup packed dried sour cherries
2 teaspoons white cloves
1 teaspoon whole coriander seeds

For the Cherry Vanilla Soda Mixer

Preheat a water bath to 160°F (71.1°C).

Lightly scrub the outside of the lemon then remove the zest with a vegetable peeler or zester. Make sure little to no pith came off as well, using a paring knife to remove any.

Combine the lemon zest with all the remaining ingredients in a sous vide bag or Mason jar then seal. Infuse in the water bath for 2 to 4 hours.

Prepare an ice bath with ½ ice and ½ water. Remove the bag or Mason jar from the water bath and place in the ice bath for 15 to 20 minutes. Strain the infusion and store in a sealed container. It will last for several weeks in the refrigerator.

Root Beer Soda Mixer Concentrate

Cooks: 160°F (71.1°C) for 1 to 3 hours • Makes: 3 cups mix

I don't drink much soda but when I do I almost always reach for root beer. It's a classic drink that has been around since the late 1800s and it's full of deep, nuanced flavors. Making it at home is easy once you obtain the ingredients, most of which I ordered online from HerbsofMexico.com.

This recipe contains no sugar, so it comes out similar to a weak bitters that I'll often serve mixed with club soda and a little honey. If you want a more traditional root beer syrup you can add 1 cup of brown sugar to the recipe, or another sweetener of your choice.

One disclaimer, in the 1960s the government removed sassafras from root beer recipes because when taken by mice in large quantities (the equivalent of five 2-liter bottles a day) the safrole in it was correlated with liver cancer. It has since been replaced by wintergreen. Of course, basil and nutmeg have safrole too, but if you are uncomfortable using it feel free to substitute it in this recipe with wintergreen.

For the Root Beer Soda Mixer
- 3 cups water
- ½ cup sassafras root
- 2 tablespoons sarsaparilla root
- 1 tablespoon birch bark
- 2 teaspoons burdock root
- 2 teaspoons licorice root
- 3 star anise pods
- 1 vanilla bean, split lengthwise
- 1 cinnamon stick

For the Root Beer Soda Mixer

Preheat a water bath to 160°F (71.1°C).

Combine all of the ingredients in a sous vide bag or Mason jar then seal. Infuse in the water bath for 1 to 3 hours.

Prepare an ice bath with ½ ice and ½ water. Remove the bag or Mason jar from the water bath and place in the ice bath for 15 to 20 minutes. Strain the infusion and store in a sealed container. It will last for several weeks in the refrigerator.

Equipment Links

There are several different kinds of equipment you can use in sous vide, and each kind has many different brands that are offering solutions. Here are some of the brands I respect most, broken down by category. The equipment used in sous vide is constantly evolving so I highly recommend checking out my online sous vide equipment pages for all the latest details at AFMEasy.com/HEquip.

Searing

Once your food is cooked you need to get a flavorful sear on it. Here are a few of the top options for accomplishing that.

Bernzomatic
Bernzomatic is the generally considered the best torch to sear sous vide food with.
www.bernzomatic.com
amzn.to/2lDsajY

Iwatani Torch
Iwatani also makes a high quality torch for searing sous vide food.
www.iwatani.com
amzn.to/2li8K8j

Searzall
The Searzall is an attachment for the Bernzomatic torch that allows for more even, gentle heating.
www.bookeranddax.com
amzn.to/2m0koBD

Lodge Cast Iron Skillet
A heavy cast iron skillet is great for searing, or to use as a base for torching your food.
www.lodgemfg.com
amzn.to/2lij4gm

All-Clad Stainless Steel Fry Pan
A high-quality, heavy stainless steel frying pan is also a wonderful way to sear your food.
www.all-clad.com
amzn.to/2mxpus8

Circulators

Immersion circulators and water baths are the backbone of sous vide. They keep the water at a set temperature and ensure your food will turn out perfectly.

Joule
The Joule is a WiFi-enabled sous vide circulator by ChefSteps that can only be controlled via a smartphone app.
www.chefsteps.com/joule
amzn.to/2ke8zX5

Sansaire
The Sansaire is a first generation circulator that is powerful and quiet.
www.sansaire.com
amzn.to/2jUCBhf

Anova
The Anova is one of the best selling sous vide circulators and comes with or without WiFi.
www.anovaculinary.com
amzn.to/2m0pfTH

Gourmia
Gourmia is a less expensive, but powerful, circulator that can also come with WiFi.
www.gourmia.com
amzn.to/2lgIdDI

Containers, Clips and Racks

There are a wide variety of containers you can use for sous vide, as well as clips and racks that help hold your food in place during the long cook times.

Cambro Container
Cambro makes several sizes of polycarbonate containers that are excellent for sous vide.
www.cambro.com
amzn.to/2lDL4Hv

Rubbermaid Container
Rubbermaid also makes several sizes of containers that work well for sous vide.
www.rubbermaid.com
amzn.to/2lDGgC0

Lipavi Container
Lipavi has a full line of containers and matching racks, along with cut lids for many circulators.
www.lipavi.com
amzn.to/2mxz66n

Uxcell Alligator Clamp
These clips are a convenient way to keep your sous vide bag attached to the container.
www.uxcell.com
amzn.to/2yBFLkN

CMS Disc Magnet
These strong magnets are a great way to hold your sous vide bags in place.
www.cmsmagnetics.com
amzn.to/2lxJgiy

Sous Vide Magnets
These magnets are silicon coated and made specifically for sous vide machines.
amzn.to/2nbr96H

Sous Vide Supreme Rack
This inexpensive rack made by Sous Vide Supreme works great in many other containers as well.
www.sousvidesupreme.com
bit.ly/2mPhvG0

Ikea Variera Rack
IKEA makes a dish holder rack that many people use in their sous vide machines to hold down their bags.
www.ikea.com
amzn.to/2mKmO7I

Sealers

There are three common ways to seal a sous vide bag. They are with a chambered vacuum sealer, an "edge-type" vacuum sealer, and a Ziploc bag.

FoodSaver
FoodSaver is the best selling edge-style vacuum sealer on the market and has many different models at multiple price points.
www.foodsaver.com
amzn.to/2lYkPOq

VacMaster
VacMaster makes several chambered vacuum sealers which are expensive but are excellent for sous vide and general food storage.
www.vacmaster.com
amzn.to/2m0rYfT

Oliso
The Oliso vacuum sealer is similar to a FoodSaver but is more compact.
www.oliso.com/shop/vacuumsealer

Ziploc
Ziploc bags are in almost everyone's kitchen and are an inexpensive way to seal food for sous vide.
ziploc.com
amzn.to/2lYx3GU

Other

Here are a few other cooking accessories I like to use or mention in the book. Some are for everyday cooking and others are great for special occasions.

PolyScience Smoking Gun
The Smoking Gun is an excellent way to add flavor and aroma to many dishes.
www.polyscience.com
amzn.to/2lDJVji

Fagor Pressure Cooker
A high-quality pressure cooker is a great way to quickly make braise-like food.
www.fagoramerica.com
amzn.to/2lnyz6T

iSi Gourmet Whip
A whipping siphon is one of my favorite kitchen tools and is wonderful for infusions, whipped cream, and foams.
www.isi.com/us/culinary
amzn.to/2mOSMzr

Cooking by Thickness

There are two ways to cook sous vide, one is based on the thickness of the food and the other is based on the desired tenderness. When cooking based on the thickness of the food it is helpful to have a reference guide to fall back on. I've combined several of the respectable sous vide charts into one easy-to-use reference.

Both methods have their uses. Thickness-based is ideal for very tender cuts cooked by people who need them done in the minimum amount of time. Tenderness-based is best for tougher cuts or people that have a range of time that they are interested in. This chapter focuses on thickness and the next is on tenderness.

Cooking by Thickness

Cooking sous vide based on thickness basically tells you the minimum time you can cook a piece of meat to ensure it is safe and comes up to temperature in the middle. It doesn't take in to account tenderizing time or any other factors.

Cooking based on thickness is how PolyScience, Baldwin, and Nathan started out as they did research on food safety.

Cooking by thickness is most often used by restaurants or home cooks who want to minimize cooking time and are using tender cuts of meat that don't need any tenderization.

Notes on the Thickness Times

The times were extrapolated from the descriptions in Baldwin's *Practical Guide to Sous Vide* as well as Nathan's tables on eGullet and a few other sources.

The times given are approximate since there are many factors that go in to how quickly food is heated. For example, the density of the food matters, which is one reason beef heats differently than chicken. To a lesser degree where you get your beef from will also affect the cooking time, and whether the beef was factory raised, farm raised, or grass-fed. Because of this, I normally don't try to pull the food out at the exact minute it is done unless I'm in a real rush.

The times shown are also the minimum times to heat or pasteurize the food. The food can be, and sometimes needs to be, left in for longer periods in order to fully tenderize the meat. If you are cooking food longer, remember that food should not be cooked at temperatures less than 131°F (55°C) for more than 4 hours.

For a printable version of these charts you can download the ruler from my website at: AFMEasy.com/HRuler.

Thickness Times for Beef, Lamb and Pork

These are the times for heating, cooling, and pasteurizing beef, lamb and other red meat, as well as pork. These times apply to most types of meat except fish, though chicken and poultry are almost always cooked to pasteurization and have been moved to their own section for clarity. If you have some other type of meat (moose, bear, rabbit, etc.) you can use these charts as well.

Heating Times for Beef, Lamb and Pork

These times specify how long it takes a piece of meat, with a particular shape, to heat all the way to the center. The center of the meat will come up to about 1° less than the water bath temperature in the time given. The final degree takes a much longer time and generally does not contribute to the final taste or texture.

While there are slight differences in the heating time for different temperatures of water baths, the times usually vary less than 5 to 10% even going from a 111°F bath to a 141°F bath (43.8°C to 60.5°C), which equates to a difference of 5 minutes every hour. I show the largest value in the chart.

Remember that you should not cook food at much less than 130°F (54.5°C) for more than 4 hours. If you want to cook a piece of food at a lower temperature, you can cut it into smaller portions so it heats more quickly. The times shown are also minimum times and food can be, and sometimes needs to be, left in for longer periods in order to fully tenderize it.

Starting Temp: Shape of Meat:	Fridge Slab	Fridge Cylinder	Freezer Slab	Freezer Cylinder
2.75" (70mm)	–	3:30	–	5:00
2.50" (63mm)	5:10	2:50	–	4:20
2.25" (57mm)	4:25	2:20	6:35	3:45
2.00" (51mm)	3:35	2:00	5:30	3:00
1.75" (44mm)	3:00	1:30	4:30	2:30
1.50" (38mm)	2:20	1:10	3:20	1:50
1.25" (32mm)	1:40	0:55	2:35	1:20
1.00" (25mm)	1:15	0:40	1:50	1:00
0.75" (19mm)	0:50	0:30	1:15	0:45
0.50" (13mm)	0:30	0:15	0:40	0:25
0.25" (6mm)	0:10	0:06	0:15	0:15

Pasteurization Times for Beef, Lamb and Pork

If you want to ensure that your food is safe to eat through pasteurization, then you can follow these sous vide times. They let you know how long you need to cook something, specifically most red meat, for it to be effectively pasteurized and safe to eat.

Like the heating and cooling times, they are not exact, but they are also on the longer side for safety reasons.

Thickness	131°F (55°C)	135°F (57°C)	140°F (60°C)
2.75" (70mm)	6:30	5:15	4:00
2.50" (63mm)	5:40	4:35	3:35
2.25" (57mm)	5:10	4:00	3:05
2.00" (51mm)	4:30	3:20	2:30
1.75" (44mm)	4:00	3:00	2:15
1.50" (38mm)	3:25	2:25	1:55
1.25" (32mm)	3:10	2:05	1:40
1.00" (25mm)	2:45	2:00	1:30
0.75" (19mm)	2:30	1:45	1:15
0.50" (13mm)	2:10	1:25	0:50
0.25" (6mm)	1:50	1:00	0:35

Cooling Times for Beef, Lamb and Pork

If you are cooking food and then storing it in the refrigerator or freezer, then these sous vide cooling times will give you the time that food needs to be in an ice bath before the center is chilled out of the danger zone.

Just like with heating, the actual temperature change isn't a big factor in the time needed to cool it. Just make sure the ice bath is at least one half ice to ensure proper cooling.

Starting Temp: Shape of Meat:	Hot Cylinder	Hot Slab
2.75" (70mm)	2:45	5:30
2.50" (63mm)	2:10	4:35
2.25" (57mm)	1:50	4:00
2.00" (51mm)	1:30	3:15
1.75" (44mm)	1:15	2:45
1.50" (38mm)	1:00	2:05
1.25" (32mm)	0:45	1:35
1.00" (25mm)	0:30	1:15
0.75" (19mm)	0:20	0:50
0.50" (13mm)	0:15	0:30
0.25" (6mm)	0:10	0:15

Thickness Times for Chicken and Poultry

Sous vide chicken is almost always cooked until it is pasteurized. For heating and cooling times you can reference the previous section.

Pasteurization Times for Chicken

The sous vide pasteurization times in the chart will ensure that the chicken is always safe to eat. These times are for chicken that has been in the refrigerator, for frozen chicken add some extra time.

Thickness	137°F (58°C)	140°F (60°C)	145°F (63°C)	149°F (65°C)
2.75" (70mm)	6:00	5:00	4:15	3:45
2.50" (63mm)	5:20	4:25	3:35	3:10
2.25" (57mm)	4:50	4:05	3:10	2:55
2.00" (51mm)	4:15	3:20	2:30	2:20
1.75" (44mm)	3:45	3:00	2:15	2:00
1.50" (38mm)	3:10	2:30	1:55	1:40
1.25" (32mm)	2:55	2:10	1:40	1:25
1.00" (25mm)	2:15	1:35	1:15	0:55
0.75" (19mm)	2:00	1:20	0:50	0:40
0.50" (13mm)	1:50	1:10	0:35	0:25
0.25" (6mm)	1:40	0:50	0:25	0:20

Heating Times for Fatty Fish

These sous vide times will help you determine how long you need to cook fatty fish in order for it to be brought up to temperature. It will not pasteurize the fish, so make sure you use high quality fish you would be comfortable eating raw.

There are slight differences in the heating time for different temperatures of water baths but they usually vary less than 5 to 10% even going from a 111°F bath to a 141°F bath (43.8°C to 60.5°C), which equates to a difference of 5 minutes every hour. I show the largest value in the chart.

The chart assumes the fish is defrosted.

Thickness	Time
2.75" (70mm)	3:50
2.50" (63mm)	3:05
2.25" (57mm)	2:40
2.00" (51mm)	2:00
1.75" (44mm)	1:40
1.50" (38mm)	1:20
1.25" (32mm)	0:55
1.00" (25mm)	0:35
0.75" (19mm)	0:21
0.50" (13mm)	0:10
0.25" (6mm)	0:05

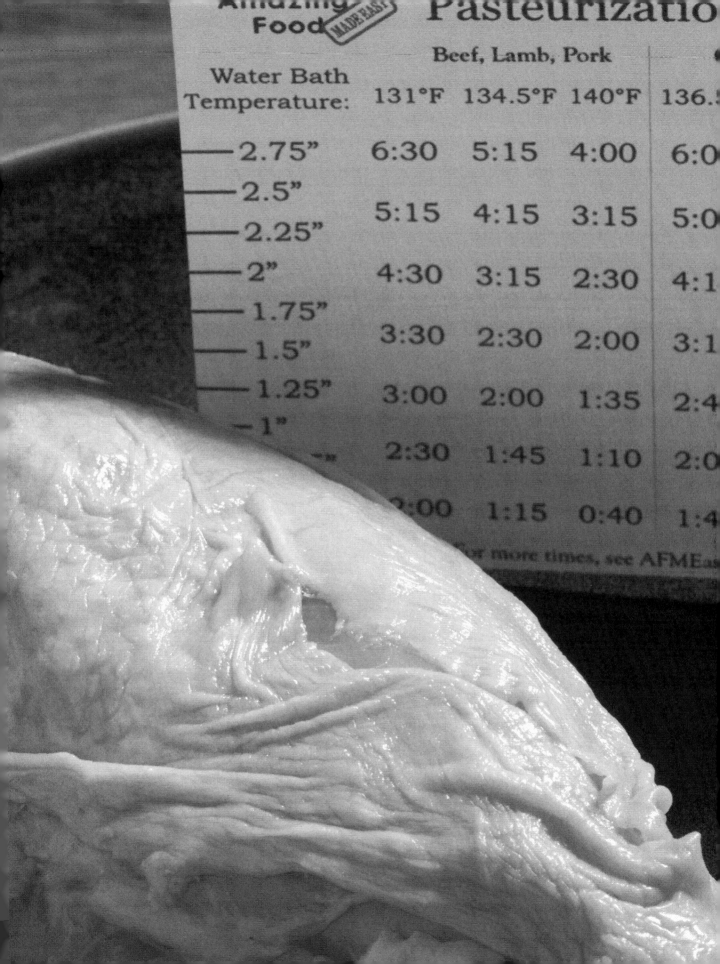

Cooking by Tenderness

Cooking by tenderness is dependent on how tender or tough the cut of meat is. Some cuts just need to be heated through while others need extended cooks of several days until they are broken down enough to enjoy.

To come up with the tenderness times I've leaned on my own experience and the reports of other people. It is important to understand that all times are estimates, as there are many factors that go in to how tough a piece of meat is. I have cooked a chuck roast for 18 hours and had it turn out too tender, and I've cooked one for 36 hours that was still tough.

The best way to get consistent results is to turn to a butcher or fish monger that you frequent so you can understand how their meat cooks.

The times given are my personal preferences and will get you in the ball park of what you are looking for. If you discover you like something cooked longer or shorter, please go with what you prefer.

Note: For more information about the ranges given, please read my in-depth blog post *Why the Range? Sous Vide Times Explained* AFMEasy.com/HRange.

Beef, Pork, Lamb and Other Meat

Most of the cuts below can have a few different options including "Steak-Like", "Tender Steak" and up to three braising entries.

Steak-Like

Following the "Steak-Like" entry will result in a final dish that has the texture and doneness of a great steak. I recommend starting with 125°F (51.6°C) for rare, 131°F (55°C) for medium rare and 140°F (60°C) for medium. You can then adjust the temperature up or down in future cooks to better match your preference.

General Doneness Range
Rare: 120°F to 129°F (49°C to 53.8°C)
Medium Rare: 130°F to 139°F (54.4°C to 59.4°C)
Medium: 140°F to 145°F (60°C to 62.8°C)
Well Done: Above 145°F (62.8°C)

For the timing, you usually will be given a specific range that I've found to work well for that cut, such as "2 to 4 hours", or "1 to 2 days".

Other timing options are "Time by Thickness" or "Pasteurize by Thickness", which indicates that this cut doesn't need tenderization, it only needs to be heated through and/or pasteurized. You can follow the charts in the Cooking by Thickness chapter for the specific times. I've used "Pasteurize by Thickness" for entries that are almost always pasteurized, but many people also pasteurize the majority of their meat to be on the safe side.

> **Warning:** If you drop the temperature much below 130°F (54.4°C) you are in the danger zone, not killing any pathogens, and shouldn't cook the food for more than an hour or two.

Tender Steak

In addition to the "Steak-Like" entry, some cuts will have a "Tender Steak" entry. These are cuts that are traditionally eaten grilled or pan fried, such as flank, sirloin, or flat iron steaks but that can also benefit from some tenderization. If you follow the "Steak-Like" entry, they will turn out very similar to the traditionally cooked version, while following the "Tender Steak" entry will result in a much more tender version of that steak.

Braise-Like

Some cuts can also be traditionally braised so I give my three favorite time and temperature combinations for them as well.

Most braise-like temperatures range from around 150°F up to 185°F (65.6°C up to 85°C). The temperatures I recommend trying first are:

- 156°F (68.8°C) for a shreddable, but still firm texture
- 165°F (73.9°C) for a more fall apart texture
- 176°F (80.0°C) for a really fall apart texture

From a timing standpoint, going from 131°F to 156°F (55°C to 68.8°C) seems to cut the cook time in half. Going above 176°F (80.0°C) seems to cut it in half again.

Beef Times and Temperatures

Blade
Steak-Like: Time by Thickness
Tender Steak: Up to 10 hours

Bottom Round
Steak-Like: For 2 to 3 days
Braise-Like:
   156°F (68.8°C) for 1 to 2 days
   165°F (73.9°C) for 1 to 2 days
   176°F (80.0°C) for 12 to 24 hours

Brisket
Steak-Like: For 2 to 3 days
Braise-Like:
   156°F (68.8°C) for 1 to 2 days
   165°F (73.9°C) for 1 to 2 days
   176°F (80.0°C) for 12 to 24 hours

Cheek
Steak-Like: For 2 to 3 days
Braise-Like:
   156°F (68.8°C) for 1 to 2 days
   165°F (73.9°C) for 1 to 2 days
   176°F (80.0°C) for 12 to 24 hours

Chuck
Pot Roast
Steak-Like: For 36 to 60 hours
Braise-Like:
   156°F (68.8°C) for 18 to 24 hours
   165°F (73.9°C) for 18 to 24 hours
   176°F (80.0°C) for 12 to 18 hours

Eye Round
Steak-Like: For 1 to 2 days
Braise-Like:
   156°F (68.8°C) for 18 to 36 hours
   165°F (73.9°C) for 18 to 36 hours
   176°F (80.0°C) for 8 to 18 hours

Flank
Bavette
Steak-Like: Time by Thickness
Tender Steak: Up to 2 days, I prefer 12 hours

Flat Iron
Steak-Like: Time by Thickness
Tender Steak: Up to 24 hours

Hamburger
Steak-Like: Pasteurize by Thickness

Hanger
Steak-Like: Time by Thickness

London Broil
Not a true cut but normally flank, chuck, or round
Steak-Like: For 18 to 60 hours
Braise-Like:
   156°F (68.8°C) for 12 to 24 hours
   165°F (73.9°C) for 12 to 24 hours
   176°F (80.0°C) for 8 to 18 hours

Porterhouse
Steak-Like: Time by Thickness

Pot Roast
Steak-Like: For 2 to 3 days
Braise-Like:
   156°F (68.8°C) for 1 to 2 days
   165°F (73.9°C) for 1 to 2 days
   176°F (80.0°C) for 12 to 24 hours

Prime Rib
Standing Rib Roast, Rib Roast
Steak-Like: Time by Thickness
Tender Steak: Up to 10 hours

Ribeye
Rib Steak, Delmonico Steak, Scotch Filet, Entrecôte
Steak-Like: Time by Thickness
Tender Steak: Up to 8 hours

Ribs
Beef Spareribs
Steak-Like: For 1 to 2 days
Braise-Like:
  156°F (68.8°C) for 18 to 36 hours
  165°F (73.9°C) for 18 to 36 hours
  176°F (80.0°C) for 8 to 18 hours

Sausage
Steak-Like: Pasteurize by Thickness

Shank
Shin
Steak-Like: For 2 to 3 days
Braise-Like:
  156°F (68.8°C) for 1 to 2 days
  165°F (73.9°C) for 1 to 2 days
  176°F (80.0°C) for 12 to 24 hours

Short Ribs
Back Ribs, Flanken Ribs
Steak-Like: For 2 to 3 days
Braise-Like:
  156°F (68.8°C) for 1 to 2 days
  165°F (73.9°C) for 1 to 2 days
  176°F (80.0°C) for 12 to 24 hours

Shoulder
Steak-Like: Time by Thickness
Tender Steak: Up to 24 hours

Sirloin
Steak-Like: Time by Thickness
Tender Steak: Up to 10 hours

Skirt
Steak-Like: Time by Thickness
Tender Steak: Up to 24 hours

Stew Meat
Various Cuts
Steak-Like: For 36 to 60 hours
Braise-Like:
  156°F (68.8°C) for 18 to 24 hours
  165°F (73.9°C) for 18 to 24 hours
  176°F (80.0°C) for 12 to 18 hours

Strip
Top Loin Strip, New York Strip, Kansas City Strip, Top Sirloin, Top Loin, Shell Steak
Steak-Like: Time by Thickness

Sweetbreads
Steak-Like: Time by Thickness

T-Bone
Steak-Like: Time by Thickness

Tenderloin
Filet mignon, Châteaubriand, Tournedo
Steak-Like: Time by Thickness

Tongue
Steak-Like: For 2 to 3 days
Braise-Like:
  156°F (68.8°C) for 1 to 2 days
  165°F (73.9°C) for 1 to 2 days
  176°F (80.0°C) for 12 to 24 hours

Top Round
Steak-Like: For 1 to 2 days
Not recommended above 145°F (62.8°C)

Tri-Tip
Steak-Like: Time by Thickness
Tender Steak: Up to 24 hours

Lamb Times and Temperatures

Arm Chop
Steak-Like: For 18 to 36 hours

Blade Chop
Steak-Like: For 18 to 36 hours

Breast
Steak-Like: For 1 to 2 days
Braise-Like:
    156°F (68.8°C) for 18 to 24 hours
    165°F (73.9°C) for 18 to 24 hours
    176°F (80.0°C) for 12 to 18 hours

Leg, Bone In
Steak-Like: Time by Thickness
Tender Steak: Up to 24 hours

Leg, Boneless
Steak-Like: Time by Thickness
Tender Steak: Up to 24 hours

Loin Chops
Steak-Like: Time by Thickness

Loin Roast
Steak-Like: Time by Thickness

Loin, Boneless
Steak-Like: Time by Thickness

Neck
Steak-Like: For 2 to 3 days
Braise-Like:
    156°F (68.8°C) for 1 to 2 days
    165°F (73.9°C) for 1 to 2 days
    176°F (80.0°C) for 12 to 24 hours

Osso Buco
Steak-Like: For 1 to 2 days
Braise-Like:
    156°F (68.8°C) for 18 to 24 hours
    165°F (73.9°C) for 18 to 24 hours
    176°F (80.0°C) for 12 to 18 hours

Rack
Steak-Like: Time by Thickness

Rib Chop
Steak-Like: Time by Thickness

Ribs
Steak-Like: For 1 to 2 days
Braise-Like:
    156°F (68.8°C) for 18 to 24 hours
    165°F (73.9°C) for 18 to 24 hours
    176°F (80.0°C) for 12 to 18 hours

Shank
Steak-Like: For 1 to 2 days
Braise-Like:
    156°F (68.8°C) for 18 to 24 hours
    165°F (73.9°C) for 18 to 24 hours
    176°F (80.0°C) for 12 to 18 hours

Shoulder
Steak-Like: For 1 to 2 days
Braise-Like:
    156°F (68.8°C) for 18 to 24 hours
    165°F (73.9°C) for 18 to 24 hours
    176°F (80.0°C) for 12 to 18 hours

Tenderloin
Steak-Like: Time by Thickness

Pork Times and Temperatures

I have replaced "Steak-Like" with "Chop-Like" so it is more accurate but please refer to the "Beef and Red Meat" intro for a full description. My recommended temperatures for "Chop-Like" pork is 135°F (57.2°C), 140°F (60°C), or 145°F (62.8°C), with 140°F (60°C) being my favorite.

Arm Steak
Chop-Like: For 1 to 2 days

Baby Back Ribs
Chop-Like: For 1 to 2 days
Braise-Like:
   156°F (68.8°C) for 18 to 24 hours
   165°F (73.9°C) for 18 to 24 hours
   176°F (80.0°C) for 12 to 18 hours

Back Ribs
Chop-Like: For 1 to 2 days
Braise-Like:
   156°F (68.8°C) for 18 to 24 hours
   165°F (73.9°C) for 18 to 24 hours
   176°F (80.0°C) for 12 to 18 hours

Belly
Chop-Like: For 2 to 3 days
Braise-Like:
   156°F (68.8°C) for 1 to 2 days
   165°F (73.9°C) for 1 to 2 days
   176°F (80.0°C) for 12 to 24 hours

Blade Chops
Chop-Like: For 8 to 12 hours

Blade Roast
Chop-Like: For 1 to 2 days
Braise-Like:
   156°F (68.8°C) for 18 to 24 hours
   165°F (73.9°C) for 18 to 24 hours
   176°F (80.0°C) for 12 to 18 hours

Blade Steak
Chop-Like: For 18 to 36 hours

Boston Butt
Chop-Like: For 1 to 2 days
Braise-Like:
   156°F (68.8°C) for 18 to 24 hours
   165°F (73.9°C) for 18 to 24 hours
   176°F (80.0°C) for 12 to 18 hours

Butt Roast
Chop-Like: For 1 to 2 days
Braise-Like:
   156°F (68.8°C) for 18 to 24 hours
   165°F (73.9°C) for 18 to 24 hours
   176°F (80.0°C) for 12 to 18 hours

Country Style Ribs
Chop-Like: For 18 to 36 hours
Braise-Like:
   156°F (68.8°C) for 9 to 18 hours
   165°F (73.9°C) for 6 to 14 hours
   176°F (80.0°C) for 4 to 9 hours

Fresh Side Pork
Chop-Like: For 2 to 3 days
Braise-Like:
   156°F (68.8°C) for 1 to 2 days
   165°F (73.9°C) for 1 to 2 days
   176°F (80.0°C) for 12 to 24 hours

Ground Pork
Pasteurize by Thickness

Ham Roast
Chop-Like: For 10 to 20 hours

Ham Steak
Chop-Like: Time by Thickness

Leg (Fresh Ham)
Chop-Like: For 10 to 20 hours

Loin Chop
Chop-Like: Pasteurize by Thickness

Loin Roast
Chop-Like: Pasteurize by Thickness

Picnic Roast
Chop-Like: For 1 to 2 days
Braise-Like:
    156°F (68.8°C) for 18 to 24 hours
    165°F (73.9°C) for 18 to 24 hours
    176°F (80.0°C) for 12 to 18 hours

Pork Chops
Chop-Like: Pasteurize by Thickness

Rib Chops
Chop-Like: For 5 to 8 hours

Rib Roast
Chop-Like: For 5 to 8 hours

Sausage
Pasteurize by Thickness

Shank
Chop-Like: For 1 to 2 days
Braise-Like:
    156°F (68.8°C) for 18 to 24 hours
    165°F (73.9°C) for 18 to 24 hours
    176°F (80.0°C) for 12 to 18 hours

Shoulder
Chop-Like: For 1 to 2 days
Braise-Like:
    156°F (68.8°C) for 18 to 24 hours
    165°F (73.9°C) for 18 to 24 hours
    176°F (80.0°C) for 12 to 18 hours

Sirloin Chops
Chop-Like: For 6 to 12 hours

Sirloin Roast
Chop-Like: For 6 to 12 hours

Spare Ribs
Chop-Like: For 1 to 2 days
Braise-Like:
    156°F (68.8°C) for 18 to 24 hours
    165°F (73.9°C) for 18 to 24 hours
    176°F (80.0°C) for 12 to 18 hours

Spleen
Chop-Like: Pasteurize by Thickness

Tenderloin
Chop-Like: Pasteurize by Thickness

Chicken and Poultry Times and Temperatures

Chicken, Turkey and Other "Well Done" Poultry

Breast
All should be pasteurized by thickness
Medium-Rare: 137°F (58°C)
Ideal: 141°F (60.5°C)
Medium-Well: 149°F (65°C)

Leg / Drumstick
Medium: 141°F (60.5°C) for 4 to 6 hours
Ideal: 148°F (64.4°C) for 4 to 6 hours
Shreddable: 165°F (73.9°C) for 8 to 12 hours

Sausage
All should be pasteurized by thickness
White Meat: 141°F (60.5°C)
Dark Meat: 148°F (64.4°C)
Mixed Meat: 141°F (60.5°C)

Thigh
Medium: 141°F (60.5°C) for 4 to 6 hours
Ideal: 148°F (64.4°C) for 4 to 6 hours
Shreddable: 165°F (73.9°C) for 8 to 12 hours

Whole Bird
Not recommended, but if you do try to spatchcock it to remove the air pocket or it could harbor bacteria during the cooking process. For all temperatures it should be pasteurized by thickness.
Medium: 141°F (60.5°C)
Medium-Well: 149°F (65°C)

Duck, Goose and "Medium Rare" Poultry

Breast
Rare: 125°F (51.6°C) by thickness
Medium-Rare: 131°F (55°C) by thickness
Medium: 140°F (60°C) by thickness

Leg
Medium-Rare: 131°F (55°C) for 3 to 6 hours
Medium: 140°F (60°C) for 3 to 6 hours
Confit: 167°F (75°C) for 10 to 20 hours

Sausage
131°F (55°C) by thickness

Thigh
Medium-Rare: 131°F (55°C) for 3 to 6 hours
Medium: 140°F (60°C) for 3 to 6 hours
Confit: 167°F (75°C) for 10 to 20 hours

Whole Bird
Not recommended, but if you do try to spatchcock it to remove the air pocket. For all temperatures it should be heated by thickness.
Medium-Rare: 131°F (55°C) for 3 to 6 hours
Medium: 140°F (60°C) for 3 to 6 hours

Eggs

The timing will change based on the size of the egg. The times below are for an average-sized American Large Grade A egg.

"Raw" Pasteurized Eggs
131°F (55°C) for 75 to 90 minutes

Soft Boiled / Poached
140°F to 145°F (60°C to 62.8°C) for 40 to 60 minutes
167°F (75°C) for 13 minutes

Semi-Hard
150°F (65.6°C) for 40 to 60 minutes

Hard Boiled
165°F (73.9°C) for 40 to 60 minutes

Fish and Shellfish Times and Temperatures

Fish

Most fish follow the below temperatures pretty well, but different fish may be preferable at different temperatures.

Warning: All of the fish you use should be high quality fish you would feel comfortable eating raw. The times and temperatures used are almost never enough to pasteurize them.

General Fish Times
All cook times should be based on the thickness, which is about:

0.5" (13mm) thick for 14 minutes
1" (25mm) thick for 35 minutes
1.5" (38mm) thick for 1 hour 25 minutes
2" (50mm) thick for 2 hours

General Fish Temperatures
Slightly Warmed: 104°F (40°C)
Firm Sashimi: 110°F (43.3°C)
Lightly Flaky and/or Firm: 120°F (48.9°C)
Very Flaky and/or Firm: 132°F (55.5°C)
Chewy: 140°F (60°C)

Shellfish

Shellfish varies greatly depending on the type you are trying to cook. Here are times and temperatures for some of the more common ones.

Crab
132°F (55.5°C) for 30 to 60 minutes
140°F (60°C) for 30 to 60 minutes

Lobster
The Serious Eats guide to lobster is a great resource.
Low Temp: 115°F (46.1°C) for 20 to 40 minutes
Medium: 122°F (50°C) for 20 to 40 minutes
Ideal: 130°F (54°C) for 20 to 40 minutes
Very Firm: 140°F (60°C) for 20 to 40 minutes
Ideal Claw: 150°F (65.5°C) for 20 to 40 minutes

Octopus
Slow Cook: 170°F (76.6°C) for 4 to 8 hours
Fast Cook: 180°F (82.2°C) for 2 to 4 hours

Scallops
122°F (50°C) for 15 to 35 minutes
131°F (55°C) for 15 to 35 minutes

Shrimp
Sushi-Like: 122°F (50°C) for 15 to 35 minutes
Tender: 131°F (55°C) for 15 to 35 minutes
Firm: 140°F (60°C) for 15 to 35 minutes

Squid
Pre-Sear: 113°F (45°C) for 45 to 60 minutes
Low Heat: 138°F (58.9°C) for 2 to 4 hours
High Heat: 180°F (82.2°C) for 1 to 2 hours

Fruit and Vegetable Times and Temperatures

Almost all vegetables are cooked at 183°F (83.9°C) or higher and all entries below assume that temperature, unless otherwise stated. Hotter temperatures will cook the vegetables more quickly, but they will basically have the same texture at the end. There is also variability in a specific type of vegetable, with both their ripeness, variety, and size having an impact. So times can vary across vegetables, even of the same type.

Acorn Squash 1 to 2 hours
Apples 1 to 2 hours
Artichokes 45 to 75 minutes
Asparagus 10 to 30 minutes
Banana 10 to 15 minutes
Beet 60 to 90 minutes
Broccoli 30 to 60 minutes
Brussels Sprouts 45 to 60 minutes
Butternut Squash 45 to 60 minutes
Cabbage 60 minutes
Carrot 45 to 60 minutes
Cauliflower
    Florets 20 to 30 minutes
    For Puree 2 hours
    Stems 60 to 75 minutes
Celery Root 60 to 75 minutes
Chard 60 to 75 minutes
Cherries 15 to 25 minutes
Corn 15 to 25 minutes
Eggplant 30 to 45 minutes
Fennel 30 to 60 minutes
Golden Beets 30 to 60 minutes
Green Beans 30 to 45 minutes
Leek 30 to 60 minutes
Onion 35 to 60 minutes

Parsnip 30 to 60 minutes
Pea Pods 30 to 40 minutes
Peaches 30 to 60 minutes
Pears 25 to 60 minutes
Pineapple 167°F (75.0°C) for 45 to 60 minutes
Plums 167°F (75.0°C) for 15 to 20 minutes
Potatoes
    Small 30 to 60 minutes
    Large 60 to 120 minutes
Pumpkin 45 to 60 minutes
Radish 10 to 25 minutes
Rhubarb 141°F (60.6°C) for 25 to 45 minutes
Rutabaga 2 hours
Salsify 45 to 60 minutes
Squash
    Summer 30 to 60 minutes
    Winter 1 to 2 hours
Sunchokes 40 to 60 minutes
Sweet Potatoes
    Small 45 to 60 minutes
    Large 60 to 90 minutes
Swiss Chard 60 to 75 minutes
Turnip 45 to 60 minutes
Yams 30 to 60 minutes
Zucchini 30 to 60 minutes

Recipe Index

Beef
Chuck Steak with Asparagus and Peppers 82
Cuban Style Beef Bowl 60
Filet Mignon with Roasted Brussels Sprouts 76
Shredded Beef with Yam Neua Sauce 81
Strip Steak with Roasted Cauliflower Puree 78
Succotash with Hanger Steak 80
Top Round Salad with Watercress and Kale 50

Bison
Bison Strip Steak Carbonara 84

Chicken
Chicken and Avocado Bowl 62
Chicken Mole in the Puebla Style 92
Chicken Tikka Masala 90
Hot and Sour Chicken Soup 40

Dairy
Sous Vide Yogurt 25

Duck
Duck and Roasted Vegetable Bowl 64
Duck Breast Salad with Cherry Vinaigrette 48

Eggs
Avocado Toast with Hard-Boiled Egg 30
Broccoli Egg Cup Bites 26
Egg White Only Egg Cup Bites 28
Shakshuka with Poached Egg Blossom 32
Veggie and Gruyère Egg Cup Bites 29

Fish and Shellfish
Citrus Cured Salmon with Fennel Carpaccio 108
Halibut with Chimichurri and Tomato Salad 110
Halibut with Melon and Wheat Berries 59
Lobster Tail with Tomato and Corn Salad 104
Mahi Mahi with Charmoula 100
Scallops with Tabbouleh Salad 112
Sea Bass with Mango Salsa 98
Shrimp and Quinoa Bowl 66
Soy Sauce Cured Pollock with Apple Salad 114
Squid Puttanesca with Squash Noodles 106
Swordfish with Bean and Corn Salad 101
Swordfish with Romesco Sauce 102
Tuna and Ginger Sesame Salad 55
Tuna Poke Bowl 70
Watermelon and Cucumber Salad with Cod 52

Fruits
Apple Bourbon-Maple Chutney 24
Oatmeal with Blueberry Compote 22
Warm Peach and Blue Cheese Salad 54

Grains
Cinnamon Raisin Oatmeal 20
Simple Sous Vide Grains 58
Sous Vide Porridge 19

Infusions
Blackberry Peach Vinegar 138
Cherry Vanilla Soda Mixer Concentrate 141
Flavors of Tuscany Olive Oil 139
Lemon Tarragon Olive Oil 140
Orange Fennel Vinegar 136
Root Beer Soda Mixer Concentrate 142

Lamb
Garlic and Parsley Lamb Chop Bowl 68
Rack of Lamb with Brussels Sprouts 88

Pork
Moroccan-Style Tajine with Pork Chops 86
Pork and Ginger Bowl 67
Pork Chops with Broccolini and Peppers 85
Tortilla Soup with Shredded Pork 42

Tofu
Harissa Marinated Tofu and Kale Bowl 72

Turkey
Turkey and Avocado Salad 47
Turkey Curry with Cauliflower Pilaf 94

Vegetables
Asparagus with Garlic-Shallot Oil 125
Beets and Goat Cheese 118
Cauliflower and Chickpeas 132
Creamy Parsnip Soup 46
Curried Butternut Squash Soup 44
Dill Pickles 122
Miso Glazed Turnips 126
Red Kuri Squash Soup 38
Sesame-Miso Bok Choy 120
Sous Vide Poached Cherry Tomatoes 128
Southwestern Sweet Potato Salad 130
Spicy Rosemary Pickled Carrots 124
Spicy Street Corn 129

About the Author

Jason Logsdon is a passionate home cook who loves to try new things, exploring everything from sous vide and whipping siphons to blow torches, foams, spheres and infusions. He has published 13 cookbooks which have sold over 60,000 copies in paperback and electronic formats. His books include a best seller that hit the #1 spot on Amazon for Slow Cooking and #2 spot on Gourmet Cooking. He also runs AmazingFoodMadeEasy.com, one of the largest modernist cooking websites, and SelfPublishACookbook.com, a website dedicated to helping food bloggers successfully navigate the self publishing process.

Did You Enjoy This Book?

Most Popular Modernist Recipes

Here are some of my most popular modernist recipes.

AmazingFoodMadeEasy.com

If you are looking for sous vide recipes, detailed equipment reviews, in-depth articles, or just some inspiration, my website has you covered.

In addition to sous vide, I also cover other aspects of modernist cooking, including the whipping siphon, making foams and gels, and even infusions and spherification. Come check out how you can expand your cooking tool kit!

Modernist Cooking Made Easy: Sous Vide

Modernist Cooking Made Easy: Sous Vide is the best selling sous vide book available and the authoritative guide to low temperature precision cooking and it will help make sous vide a part of your everyday cooking arsenal.

The bulk of this book is the more than 85 recipes it contains. Designed so you can skim the recipes, looking for something that inspires you, or turn to a specific recipe to learn all about how to cook the cut of meat it features.

Modernist Cooking Made Easy: The Whipping Siphon

The whipping siphon is probably my second favortie tool after my sous vide machine. There are so many interesting and inspirational things you can do with it and my book focuses on the three main uses: Foaming, Infusing, and Carbonating. It delivers the information you need to understand how the techniques work and provides you with over 50 recipes to illustrate these techniques while allowing you to create amazing dishes that will delight everyone that tries them!

Modernist Cooking Made Easy: Infusions

The ultimate guide to crafting flavorful infusions using both modernist and traditional techniques. Exploring this process allows you to create many wonderful dishes, from custom cocktails and personalized sodas to flavorful vinaigrettes and sauces.

Discover how to create vibrant and amazing infusions that will amaze your family and friends!

Made in the USA
San Bernardino, CA
25 February 2020